Suburban ROGER KEIL [ED.]
Constellations

Suburban Constellations

ROGER KEIL [ED.]

Governance, Land, and
Infrastructure in the
21st Century

1   FOUNDATIONS

2   THEMES

3 ESSAYS AND IMAGES

4 REGIONS

ACKNOWLEDGMENTS

Roger Keil

This book project was supported by the Social Sciences and Humanities Research Council of Canada through funding from the Major Collaborative Research Initiative (MCRI) "Global suburbanisms: governance, land, and infrastructure in the 21st century (2010-2017)". It marks the halfway point of that initiative and gives us a chance to showcase our work so far. We gratefully acknowledge this support. I am thankful for the strong endorsement this book received from the Steering Committee of the MCRI and the unfailing enthusiasm that my colleagues, the Team Leaders of the various sub-areas of research brought to their chapters for the volume. I am also humbled by the wonderful contributions made by our partners, especially the National Film Board of Canada and the Greater Toronto Suburban Working Group, as well as the artists, photographers, and filmmakers who shared their work for this book. As always, a special thanks goes to Sara Macdonald, the coordinator of the MCRI, whose tireless efforts hold our large international organization together.

My appreciation goes to Susanne Rösler and Philipp Sperrle at jovis, who have been wonderful to work with throughout the process. Their professionalism and expertise must be credited for the quality of the product you have in hand.

Lastly, I would like to express my sincere gratitude to David Fleischer and Imelda Nurwisah, who worked with me in Toronto for several months to edit texts, correspond with authors, and contribute ideas to the book. David has a way with words. His stoic professionalism and wit made it look easy to work with a large number of authors with such an immense diversity of styles and topics. Imelda's judgment and persistence was indispensible in helping me select images and illustrations, in designing concepts for the sections and in finally putting it all together with painstaking patience. She kept me straight and several raisings of eyebrows at various occasions saved the book from potential visual misadventures I might have followed through with, if it were not for her candid advice.

I am honored by having been able to put *Suburban Constellations* together with the help of such special people. As is common to say, all flaws and insufficiencies contained in the book remain my responsibility.

Roger Keil
Toronto
June 2013

WELCOME TO THE SUBURBAN REVOLUTION

Roger Keil

In a world that is now more than half urban, New York City is the most urban place you can find. Manhattan. It evokes images of a forest of high-rise buildings, canyons of streets, massive pedestrian presence in noisy streetscapes, and so forth. But even New York now is one of the most suburbanized metropolitan regions in the world. Fixing our view on Manhattan can lead to a certain myopia. While significant, the traditional core of the Western world's most well-known city is only one among many centers there and clearly just one spike in the horizontalized landscape of New York's urban region, which stretches into several states and across many municipal boundaries. It also, as we now know, is not the only model of global metropolitanity but increasingly joined, rivaled, and superseded in defining our urban worlds by the emerging global cities of the likes of Shanghai, Sao Paulo, Mumbai, Lagos, just to name a few.

Driven by an oscillating dialectic of growth and decline, urbanization produces many competing forms of production of space. Suburbanization is one of them. A study of urbanization patterns in the United States has found that American society is becoming more metropolitan and that the new metropoles in that country are more diverse and more complex than their predecessors.[1]

In fact, we might now speak about living in an era of post-suburbanization where the suburbs as the newly built subdivisions at the city's edge are fading into memory and give way to complex, variably scaled, functionally differentiated, and socioeconomically mixed metropolitan structures that *contain* rather than *constrain* natures.[2]

But the physical suburbs are as resilient as the concept that denotes them. It is remarkable that just a few years after they were considered ground zero of the global financial crisis, suburbs have once again attained dreamworld status as their image is projected onto a future that vacillates between climate change denial and the virtuous realization that adaptation to the challenges of global warming has to begin in the most unsustainable place of all: the North American suburb.[3]

The very concept of suburb or suburban has recently received renewed attention. Taxonomies and lexicons of suburbanization have been developed. "The suburb" has been in the center of these considerations.[4]

In contrast to these important contributions, this book attempts a less defining and more inquisitive approach. The book advances a simple definition of suburbanization as the combination of an increase in non-central city population and economic activity, as well as urban spatial expansion. Suburbanism(s) refers to a suburban way of life. But we are less interested in laying out the conceptual boundaries of a thing called "suburb" and more keen on contextualizing the continuous suburbanization of our world in a general project of urban theory building. Inspired by Henri Lefebvre's work on the "urban revolution" and a critical reading of subsequent conversations about "planetary urbanization," the book turns our theoretical feelers out from the center and examines the "suburban revolution."[5]

Much of what goes for "urbanization" today is not what was seen as such in classical terms of urban extension. Rather, it is now generalized *sub*urbanization. In this sense, the essays below contribute to creating an opening beyond the traditional dichotomies of urban studies. "Global suburbanization" is by no means intended to reify and mark differences between the category of "suburb" and the rest of the dimensions through which general urbanization moves ahead.[6] In this sense, the book might be considered part of what Merrifield calls a "reloaded urban studies [that] suggests a thorough reframing of the urban question, of dealing adequately with the ontological question, that of being in the world, of being in an urban world. Within this conceptualization we need to dispense with all the old chestnuts between North and South, between developed and 'underdeveloped' worlds, between urban and rural, between urban and regional, *between city and suburb*, and so forth."[7] There is some relationship here, if not in intention, at least in the direction of the approach, with authors such as Dear and Dahmann who have proposed that "there is no longer such a thing as suburbanization, understood as a peripheral accretion in a center-dominated urban process."[8] Therefore, the book is as much a specific intervention into suburban debates as it is a contribution to a rejuvenated conversation on urban theory overall.[9] The essays in this book share the assumption that much if not most of what counts as urbanization today is actually peripheral.

In reloading urban studies via the suburbs, it needs to be admitted, at the outset, that critical urban theory has traditionally not held things suburban in high regard. The left's disdain for suburbs has been particularly, and understandably palpable: David Harvey made his displeasure with the periphery public at a meeting at the height of the world financial crisis in 2010 where he is quoted as calling even New York "suburban" and devoid of "urbanity."[10] Mike Davis, in his landmark *City of Quartz*, saved some of his harshest comments for the politics of homeowners in the suburban San Fernando Valley.[11] The critique of the suburbs, of course, points back to Baron Haussmann's revamping of Paris that sanitized the inner city and expelled the proletariat to the margins, and created a blueprint for generations of subsequent waves of gentrification.

We are not proposing, in the present book, to depart from the suspicions traditionally expressed towards the urban periphery, but we invite the reader to join us in reevaluating the suburban revolution we are currently experiencing as an important part of the materiality of the urban[12] through which we need to rethink and reload urban theory today.

The global suburban landscape now has a kaleidoscopic appearance. The apparent conceptual borders established by the geographic regions in the last part of this book are deceptive. There is much blurring and bleeding among and between the different world regions. In a post-colonial, post-suburban world, the forms, functions, relations, etc. of one suburban tradition get easily merged, refracted, and fully displaced in and by others elsewhere, near or far. Our optics has changed accordingly and we have collectively been challenged to abandon historically privileged spots for observing urbanization.[13] That includes both the privilege of the urban center and the privilege of the Global North, long considered — and inherently treated — as the norm in trajectories of global urbanization.

We speak once again about suburbs and suburbanization. But in contrast to earlier periods when those forms of human settlement appeared new and were cast as either the stuff of dreams or nightmares, we now have reason to inspect the suburban as a historically evolving human geography in which more questions are posed than answers given. If being urban is increasingly the shared condition of our humanity, for many if not most of us, this takes place in what we would recognize as a suburban space. So why, and how do we speak about suburbs and suburbanization in 2013?

A recent collection of essays in a Canadian cultural studies journal is introduced as a challenge to the idea, put forward by the great urbanist Lewis Mumford in 1961, that the suburb is "a thing of the past." Much more, the editors put forward the notion of "dwelling in transition," drawing "attention to both the physical changes in the peripheries of cities and to the need to revisit the conceptual armature with which urban and cultural theory approach suburbs."[14] The latter concern is on the mind of many in that special issue of *Public*. Two essays in particular set out to decode the major 2010 statement, delivered as both social commentary and art, by Montreal's Arcade Fire in their appropriately named hit album *The Suburbs*. Ian Balfour is critical but admits that The Arcade Fire's is not "the snotty downtowner's view of the impossible banality of the suburbs, the sort of posture that imagines Philistinism to permeate the water like fluoride."[15] In fact, says Balfour, "[m]ore and more the world comes to the suburbs and so the suburbs are, more and more,

The 2013 anniversary issue of
The New Yorker.
Source: Simon Grenier

the world: the periphery is not peripheral."[16] Riffing on the same theme, I conclude in my contribution to the volume that "the group's album is a major accomplishment that moves the suburbs from their marginal role in arts production into the core of our urban existence today" and cite in support the *Toronto Star*'s Ben Rayner who claims that the song cycle of *The Suburbs* "posits the transitory nature of our pre-fab satellite cities as cause for existential concern."[17]

Keeping with the hipster-looks-outward theme for a moment, let's consider the cover image of the February 2013 anniversary issue of *The New Yorker*, perhaps the most iconic metropolitan publication around. It shows a "Williamsburg hipster," the defining indicator species of gentrifying urbanity, on the other, suburban side of the river, (or perhaps on Liberty Island, at the foot of the Statue of Liberty), separated by water, with only a faint reference to the skyline of Manhattan. The image is the classical *New Yorker* dandy in reverse including a reference to the monocle! But the hipster's red cap also points to the symbolic *bonnet de coton* image of the French revolution. Will the Right to the City have to be claimed once more from the far bank of the river? And perhaps from even farther afield in the (sub) urbanized region?

Relatedly, Ralph Martin, an American author living in Berlin tells the story of the rush of fellow Berliners to the Brandenburg countryside's picturesque small towns after the fall of the Wall. A failed experiment, as the urbanites' country cousins seemed less than welcoming, but it provides the blueprint to understand the alleged trend among New Yorkers to turn their backs on the city and to look for redemption in the exurban towns of Hudson and Beacon. Their quest for "country cool" bohemia is prompting the "Brooklynization of Upstate New York.[18] The trend was confirmed when Alex Williams published a small piece in the *New York Times* fashion section that discovers "cosmopolitan bohemia … along the Metro-North Railroad, roughly 25 miles north of Williamsburg, Brooklyn, in the suburb of Hastings-on-Hudson, N.Y."[19] Miller's post invited criticism and ridicule, sarcasm and disbelief, but in the end kick-started a broader debate about the categories with which we view the city and the country.[20]

This inversion of the urban and the creative, and above all of hipsterdom, is new in an age where all things urban are to prevail, where compactness and density are the buzzwords, or better battle cries of the high priests of urbanity (although the Beat Generation and the Hippies had their fascination with the open space beyond the city and the open road but never with the suburbs).

And it is not just hipsters that are on the move. In the United States, the classical land of white middle-class, tract housing suburbia, significant change is under way. The suburbs are becoming less middle class and more non-white and immigrant. In a book that may be to this decade what Joel Garreau's *Edge City* was to the 1990s, Alan Ehrenhalt examines "the new suburbia" of cities like Atlanta, Chicago, or Houston, where he observes: "the most powerful demographic events of the past decade were the movement of African Americans out of central cities… and the settlement of immigrant groups in suburbs, often ones many miles distant form downtown."[21] Even the most well-known voice of unequivocal downtown, Jane Jacobs-style boosterism, Richard Florida, has admitted that:

> It's not just our cities and urban cores that are changing; our suburbs have, too — and to such an extent that the very categories of urban and suburban are becoming increasingly outmoded. More and more suburban households are made up of singles, empty nesters, or retirees. Even families with children are seeking a more compact, less sprawling, less car-dependent way of life. …But at their best, cities and suburbs are coming to look more and more alike — suburban shopping districts are walkable and rich with amenities like cafés and galleries; urban "strollervilles" are filled with young families. The most successful suburban and urban neighborhoods both have good transit, mixed uses, and green spaces; most important, they foster the interactions from which vital communities are built.[22]

Where Florida sees urbanity, opportunity and growth, others see crisis, gentrification, and social segregation. Researchers at the University of Toronto, for example, have recast the inner suburbs of that Canadian city as a racialized "Third City" of increasing poverty, insecure tenancy, and new immigration status.[23] Be that as it may, the conversation on suburbia has turned from its role as derivative and substandard, even pathological form of modern living to a place where worlds collide, where futures are made, where urban change has to be explained.

The suburbs have historically been the terrain of the conservative, sometimes escapist urbanist fantasies of the more privileged. Both the Fordist regime of accumulation and the neoliberal period have seen the suburban as a strategic ground for cementing the power of the upper middle classes in society.[24] But suburbs have not always been the domain of the rich and powerful (or the middle classes). In the 1920s, for example, before the American model of suburbia became the norm for peripheral urban development, socialist city builders in Europe discovered the urban peripheries of the nineteenth-century city as the space for projection of reformist or even revolutionary designs. In the best of cases, like in the New Frankfurt built under the direction of architect Ernst May, this type of working class suburbanization has been among the most sustainable and livable neighborhoods created in the twentieth century. In the worst cases, these projects left us with legacies of tower blocks that have been neglected by housing corporations that owned them, populations that abandoned them, and governments that underdeveloped them.

Among the big storylines in historic and current suburbanization are governance, land, and infrastructure. All three will be discussed in various chapters in the book. Governance is central as suburbanization and democratization have often been linked ideologically (as much as suburbs have also been criticized for destroying the very public spaces on which democratic affairs so centrally rely). Land is the first commodity that is produced before we can even speak about suburbanization as a real process. Its production is key to the extension of cities. Infrastructures are both preconditions for and always lacking in the rapidly extending settlements around the world. Suburbs have often been punching above their weight class when it comes to providing regional infrastructures. Often devoid of the benefits of prime network spaces concentrated on inner cities, they have been the classical location of airports, warehouses, large factories, trucking facilities, slaughterhouses, prisons, university expansions, logistics centers, and other large-scale infrastructures that would not be tolerated in the pristine spaces of the "last mile" in the glamour zones of the creative downtowns.

While the state and the market have been the big players in building and rebuilding suburbs over time, the periphery has also been a fertile ground for self-built urbanism. From the working class suburbs of Toronto in the early decades of the twentieth century to the *geçekondu* of Istanbul and the pop-up urbanism of squatter settlements in Africa or Asia today, individuals and communities have universally employed sweat equity to build residential neighborhoods in the geographical margins of cities.[25] In fact, perhaps Cape Town's Mitchell's Plain more than Philadelphia's Levittown is the true icon of contemporary suburbanization. This also leads to a central point this book makes: the inclusion of urbanization in the Global South in the debate on global suburbanism(s) is not a mere addition of more empirical cases to an existing script of peripheral expansion. It is the acknowledgment that the script of urban theorizing has to be rewritten from scratch. The suburbs are a good place to start that intellectual journey. It is from the emerging geographies of non-European and non-American (sub)urbanity that the architectures of urban theory await rebuilding.[26]

The reevaluation of suburbs proposed in this edited volume proceeds in three topical and methodological areas. Based on a major, multiyear research initiative that involves all contributors, but extends to fifty scholars and many more students overall worldwide, we are interested in four intertwined areas of suburban studies. In the first part, we present some foundational thinking on suburbanization. This includes three topical areas — governance, land, and infrastructure — as well as an essay on everyday suburbanisms.

The following sections elaborate on those foundational themes with more specialized accounts of suburban forms, redevelopment, risk, boundaries, water, sewage, and transportation infrastructures.

These sectoral portraits lead into a section on essays and images on mapping suburbanization, high-rises in the suburbs, and a planning experiment in suburban Toronto, the Greater Toronto Suburban Working Group.

Lastly, the book presents a global tour of suburbanization and suburbanisms with stops in Africa, India, China, Australia, North America, Latin America, and Europe.

I borrowed the general idea and structure of *Suburban Constellations* from Matthew Gandy's previous volume, *Urban Constellations*.[27] I am very grateful to Matthew for allowing us to reuse and suburbanize his concept for this book. While different in scope and approach, the present book takes up the format of presenting smaller essays, shorter interventions and interdisciplinary perspectives that Gandy's earlier Benjamin- and Kracauer-inspired volume engaged. We hope to have assembled an equally successful mélange of intellectual and artistic work in this book, which I invite you to enter with me now.

Endnotes

1   Hanlon, B./Short, J.R./ Vicino, T.J. *Cities and Suburbs: New Metropolitan Realities in the US.* New York: Routledge. 2010.

2   Sieverts, T. "Cities Without Cities." In: *Urban Design Quarterly.* 92(41). 2004.

3   Ross, A. *Bird on Fire: Lessons from the World's Least Sustainable City.* Oxford: Oxford University Press. 2011.

4   Harris, R. "Meaningful Types in a World of Suburbs." In: Clapson, M./ Hutchinson, R. (eds.): *Suburbanization in Global Society.* Bingley, England: Emerald. 2010. p. 15–50.
Forsyth, A. "Defining Suburbs." In: *Journal of Planning Literature.* 27(3). 2012. p. 270-281.

5   Lefebvre, H. *The Urban Revolution.* Minneapolis: University of Minnesota Press. 2003.
Brenner, N./Schmid, C. "Planetary Urbanisation." In: Gandy, M. (ed.): *Urban Constellations.* Berlin: Jovis. 2011. p. 10–13.

6   Merrifield, A. 2012. *Whither Urban Studies?* http://citiesmcr.wordpress.com/2012/12/10/whither-urban-studies/ . 08.01.13. See also Schafran, A. "Discourse and Dystopia, American Style: The Rise of "Slumburbia" in a Time of Crisis." In: *City.* 2013. 17(2).

7   Merrifield, 2012. Op.cit. (emphasis mine).

8   Dear, M./N.Dahmann, Urban Politics and the Los Angeles School of Urbanism, In: Judd, D.R./Simpson, D. (eds.): *The City Revisited: Urban Theory from Chicago, Los Angeles, New York.* Minneapolis: University of Minnesota Press. 2011.

9   Judd, D.R./Simpson, D. (eds.): *The City Revisited: Urban Theory from Chicago, Los Angeles, New York.* Minneapolis: University of Minnesota Press. 2011.

10 Lindsay, G. 2010. *David Harvey's Urban Manifesto: Down With Suburbia; Down With Bloomberg's New York.* http://www.fastcompany.com/1673037/david-harveys-urban-manifesto-down-suburbia-down-bloombergs-new-york. 14.02.13.

11 Davis, M. *City of Quartz: Excavating the Future in Los Angeles.* London: Verso. 1990.

12 Prigge, W. (ed.) *Die Materialität des Städtischen : Stadtentwicklung und Urbanität im gesellschaftlichen Umbruch.* Basel, Boston: Birkhäuser. 1987.

13 Roy, A. "Governing the Postcolonial Suburbs," In: Hamel, P./ Keil, R. (eds.): *Suburban Governance: A Global View.* University of Toronto Press. Forthcoming.

14 Logan, S./Marchessault, J./ Prokopow, M. "Suburbs, Dwelling in Transition." In: *Public 43.* 2011. p. 10-11.

15 Balfour, I. "Suburbs of the Mind." In: *Public 43.* 2011. p. 157.

16 Ibid,. p. 156.

17 Keil, R. "Global Suburbanization: The Challenge of Researching Cities in the 21st Century." *Public 43.* 2011. p. 60.

18 Martin, R. "Vergesst die Großstadt." In: *Frankfurter Allgemeine Sonntagszeitung.* January 27, 2013. p. 41.

19 Williams, A. "Creating Hipsturbia." In: *The New York Times,* February 15, 2013; available at http://www.nytimes.com/2013/02/17/fashion/creating-hipsturbia-in-the-suburbs-of-new-york.html?_r=0&adxnnl=1&adxnnlx=1361279203-X/HjVaicsfj6qG6MDonofg 19.02.13.

20 See for example, R.Keil, "What's With All the Hype about Hipsturbia?", http://suburbs.apps01.yorku.ca/2013/02/19/whats-with-all-the-hype-about-hipsturbia/ 20.02.13.

21 Ehrenhalt, A. *The Great Inversion and the Future of the American City.* New York: Alfred A. Knopf. 2012. p. 6.
& Garreau, J. *Edge City: Life on the New Frontier.* Anchor.1992.

22 Florida, R. "The Fading Differentiation Between City and Suburb." In: *UrbanLand.* 2013. http://urbanland.uli.org/Articles/2013/Jan/FloridaSuburbs#.URG4TkG3dYJ.twitter; 08.02.13.

23 Hulchanski, J. D. *The Three Cities Within Toronto: Income Polarization Among Toronto's Neighbourhoods, 1970-2005.* Toronto: Cities Centre, University of Toronto. 2010.

24 Peck, J. "Neoliberal Suburbanism: Frontier Space." In: *Urban Geography.* 32(6). 2011. p. 884–919.

25 Harris, R. *Unplanned Suburbs. Toronto's American Tragedy, 1900–1950.* Baltimore: Johns Hopkins University Press. 1996.

26 See, for example, McGee's contribution in this volume and Roy, A. "Governing the Postcolonial Suburbs." In: Hamel, P./Keil, R. (eds.): *Suburban Governance: A Global View.* University of Toronto Press, forthcoming.

27 Gandy, M. (ed.): *Urban Constellations.* Berlin: Jovis. 2011.

1

FOUNDATIONS

SUBURBANIZATION IN THE TWENTY-FIRST-CENTURY WORLD

Terry McGee

Istanbul: New centers —
new peripheries (2009)
Source: Roger Keil

Two premises shape the argument of this intervention. First, is the need to understand that the processes of social, political and economic change that drive the global urbanization process in the contemporary capitalist system are creating ongoing inequality both within, and between, rural and urban areas. Second, that as a consequence of this inequality there is increasing socioeconomic diversity in twenty-first century urban areas, which means that the historically persistent spatially derived images of cities need to be reexamined. This fact, as Roy reminds us in her study: "[the] messy fringes of Calcutta [are] an indication of how urban politics is constitutive of inevitably different trajectories of urbanization, such that it is impossible to deduce social outcomes from seeming regularities in spatial forms."[1] One of the unique realities of the twenty-first century is the fact that the majority of the earth's population lives in urban places. This century could well be the final phase of a transition from rural to urban life, which has been occurring since 5,000 BC. From that time, urban settlements began to proliferate but it is only since the late eighteenth century — with the development of new sources of power, technological innovations in transport and industrial technology — that urbanization has accelerated in the developed regions of the world to reach levels of 70 to 80 percent today.

For much of the rest of the globe, which is inhabited by two-thirds of the world's population, this accelerated phase of urbanization has occurred later, particularly in the latter half of the twentieth century, and while some have reached levels of urbanization similar to that of the developed countries (e.g., Japan, Brazil) a large part of the rest of the developing world, now labeled the "Global South," is still characterized by rapid urban growth.

This region is dominated by some of largest and most populated countries in the world (i.e., China, India, Pakistan, Bangladesh, Indonesia, Nigeria) which together with other countries of the "Global South" have low to medium levels of urbanization and make up two-thirds of the world's population. This means much of the urban increase that will occur in the Global South in the twenty-first century will involve a much greater volume of population increase than that which characterized the developed counties during their earlier urban transformation in the nineteenth and early twentieth centuries.

Global urbanization in the twenty-first century will be dominated by two trends. First, in the highly urbanized countries in which the major challenges are responding to the prevailing deindustrialization of urban centers, urban cores will be restructured, with an increase in service employment, slower population growth and an aging population, persistent structural unemployment, and the persistence of casual labor, which has been labeled the "precariat."[2] This situation will be exacerbated by the need to retrofit the infrastructure of nineteenth-century cities to face the needs of the twenty-first century world.

Secondly, the rapidly urbanizing countries of the Global South will see even greater challenges. These arise from the rapid population growth and volume of much younger populations, coupled with problematic economic growth as a consequence of global economic volatility and increasing competition. In this situation, informal employment may well persist in the face of structurally generated unemployment in the formal sector.

These global urban challenges will occur within the context of an increasingly integrated global system occurring at a "… new phase of global capitalism, its strategic spaces and exclusions"[3] driven by increased connectivity and interaction in urban space. This vision rests upon a recognition that globalization creates new, more rapid forms of transport and communication, more penetrative global circuits of capital that operate in the service, production and consumptions sectors and "transcending networks" that reshape urban systems and urban space both at the global, national and sub-national level. This is most clearly seen in the emergence of "global cities" such as Tokyo, New York, and London and the growth of mega-urban city regions that are part of the flows of this system. This process is buttressed by a neoliberal ideology that privileges the market system and seeks to deregulate the international and national regulatory environments.

These overarching features of the global urban system frame any discussion of the features of the variegated individual urban places at the national level that range from mega-urban regions approaching the largest in the world to the smallest of market towns. Despite great diversity, most of the larger urban places have, over the last fifty years, been characterized by similar patterns of spatial expansion and growth characterized by the restructuring of city cores and expansion into surrounding urban hinterlands. The result is an increase in non-core populations and economic activity that is perceived generically as suburbanization and has been labeled "extended urban space."[4]

Increasingly, a major component of the population of these mega-urban regions lives outside the city cores often comprising more than two-thirds of the region's population. Past theory has attempted to universalize these realities of urban spaces by creating zonal models, drawn mainly from the North American experience, of core cities with peripheral and mixed rural-urban zones on the margins of urban places but such models are increasingly less relevant to the urban centers of the twenty-first century.

But in a contradictory manner, this "space of flows" integrating urban space is also creating intra-urban socioeconomic disparities between the core cities and the peripheries of urban spaces that emerge as a major fracture zone, posing challenges for improvements in the government and management of urban places. Often, the analysis of this process privileges city cores by emphasizing the role they play as "international gateways," which are major transport nodes, locations of higher order services, and the locus of national political power. This means that the economic and social contributions of peripheries to the overall performance of mega-urban regions are downplayed. Too much emphasis is placed in public policy perceptions of the "difficulties" that the "messy urban fringes" present to the performance and image of the urban spaces as a modern symbol of progress in the global economy. This approach undervalues the complex interaction between the expansion of urban activity into the non-urban peripheries and the global and national system. Let alone their importance

in local urban regions. This means that "decentralized urban space" rather than being a homogenous spatial zone is perceived as a "fractured urban space."

As a general rule, I would argue that suburbs should be regarded as one part of the fabric of housing, commerce, and industry in contemporary global urban settlements. This statement does not deny the fact that suburbs existed as part of urban formations in preceding historical periods, but recognizes that they have become an important part of urban formations, particularly in the twentieth century and first decade of the twenty-first century. Definitions of suburbs are diverse, reflecting economic and cultural variations between societies. But a key element in the current era is that this type of settlement is given over largely to residential uses. Of course at many times in history, residential housing has been combined with economic activities. Indeed it has been argued that this was a ubiquitous feature of the preindustrial city.[5]

Another component in this definition is the conventional wisdom that suburbs are characterized by single-family homes located on individual lots sought after by families because they provide a social environment supportive of family life.[6] This Western-centric assumption is challenged in the world by the growth of extended family residences that are also increasing in the developed world as "ethno-burbs" emerge.[7]

A persistent element of the definition of suburbs is that they are generally found outside the city core. They stretch from city core boundaries in decreasing densities as urban settlements grow and expand. In many cases, but not all, they are driven by the access that automobiles provide to work, educational and social networks.[8] Finally, it is often assumed that suburbs are dormitory suburbs in which income earners commute to other places, particularly the

Istanbul: Youthful Gecekondu
dwellers (2009)
Source: Roger Keil

above: Istanbul: Hillside residential settlement, commercial
development (2009)
Source: Roger Keil

below: Istanbul: new residential
development — Asian side
(2009)
Source: Roger Keil

central city for jobs but at this time global suburbanization is characterized by an increase in employment in suburbs. In recent years, much attention has been focused on the outer ring of settlement penetrating the rural fringe. In the United States, this type of settlement is called exurban and continues a trend that had begun with the creation of holiday homes in these rural fringes.

All this diversity of suburban form is very confusing and difficult to generalize about, or handle, in a cross-cultural or transnational manner. In this intervention I want to illustrate this by the example of squatter settlements in the Global South. Some years ago I found myself grappling with a difficult category of housing, "squatter settlements" often referred to "illegal housing," said to be the consequence of "poverty" and generally assumed to be an ubiquitous part of the urbanization process in developing countries.[9]

Like "suburbs," a review of the literature on "squatter settlements" indicated that apart from the issue of "illegality," the features of "squatter settlements" were as diverse as those of "suburbs." They ranged from Jakarta's *gelandongan* (street dwellers), in which a sarong was a "roof," to the street pavement dwellers of Calcutta, to the invaders of "rust-belt" industrial locations in São Paulo and to long established squatter settlements that existed with various hues of "illegality" in the interstices of core cities and their outer suburbs.

The types of housing were equally diverse, ranging from street sleepers to housing constructed from recycled materials such as tin, canvas, and wood to "upgraded housing" characterizing, for example, some of the inner cities of Brazil. Demographically, despite assumptions of the dominance of single person households, many surveys showed that families dominated this form of housing. Locationally, they were scattered throughout the residential fabric of the urban areas. Economically they were also quite diverse; while low-income families dominated, they were not all poor and in many cases included those who could be described as lower-middle class, as I found in my surveys of Malay communities in Kuala Lumpur in the early 1960s.[10] In long-established settlements, they had begun to acquire the consumption items such as privately owned transport, kitchen consumer items, and TVs that are said to be part of the "suburban dream." So is it possible that squatter settlements, recently portrayed by Mike Davis as one symptom of the ongoing urban global crisis of the developing world, will soon be labeled as suburbs?[11]

This brief diversion into the world of "squatters" highlights the dilemma I have with the concept of "suburbia" as it has grown out of the Anglo-Euro experience. Indeed in many countries, suburbs have been ideologically privileged under the banner of neoliberalism that stresses the virtues of the unregulated market, and private property ownership resting on the "home" as a major source of consumption.[12] Thus, the suburban growth in the US was accelerated by the increase in unregulated fiscal markets in the eighties and nineties. Decentralization of political control (often associated with a decrease in fiscal transfers to municipalities) forced them to act in an entrepreneurial manner to increase city revenues, building alliances with many sectors of the housing industry.

In looking at the issues of squatters I asked why they became a category in the housing fabric of urban settlements. My answer was simple:

-The residential housing industry in the urban market economies of the developing world was, at this time, uninterested in developing a housing market for lower income communities. This was most obvious in developing countries with where government support for low–income housing was lacking and the greatest profits were drawn the market of upper-income and middle-class populations.

-The housing industry, ranging from the suppliers to developers, contractors, the real estate sector, and the financial institutions that invest in housing, was almost exclusively focused on providing housing for middle- and upper- income housing markets.

-Financial institutions were unwilling to provide housing loans for the poor and the lower middle class.

-A combination of increasing land prices in the inner cities and environmental and security problems combined with lower land and property prices in the urban periphery, providing incentives to the middle and upper income communities to move out of the inner cities.

-State and urban governments were complicit in this process, focusing on the provision of an infrastructure of roads and public services that were necessary to serve the housing the middle- and upper- income communities.[13]

Thus lower-income groups of urban society were forced to spontaneously self-generate housing wherever they could find accessible land in the interstices of existing settlements or on the peripheries. Such settlements often had low levels of public service provision, which was provided by local informal delivery systems. Indeed, in many cases a parallel housing industry grew up as squatter settlements became a very important part of the informal economy of the cities of the developing world.

As urbanization levels increased, the existence of squatter settlements presented challenges to the governments of rapidly developing countries, as urban land prices rose and low-income, higher density housing was introduced. Such was the case among some of the rapidly growing urban city states of East Asia, such as Singapore and Hong Kong. But this was necessitated, at least in part, by the restructuring that was going on in the cities. Urban governments and developers needed the squatter land for commercial redevelopment and higher income housing. Thus squatter communities were regarded as suburbs that got in the way of development; that is, of neoliberal development. In short, suburbs in the developing world have become increasingly identified with a neoliberal ideology that produces a particular form of development. In an age of rapidly increasing urbanization and challenges to global environmental and economic sustainability, the neoliberal idea of suburbs becomes increasingly unsustainable.

To conclude, I would argue that suburbs are best defined as a category of settlement that is one of the many types of the built environment of housing settlement types, commercial and industrial spaces, as well as infrastructures that include high-rise apartments, town houses, condominiums, family homes, and illegal settlements that are now part of the emerging fabric of an urbanized world. There is no evidence that this form of suburbia reflects a universal style of life that can be identified as "suburbanism." To the contrary it seems increasingly evident that they exhibit at a global, national, and local level increasing diversity and hybridity which is both a strength and challenge for the new urban theories that are emerging in the twenty-first century.

Endnotes

1   Roy, A. *City Requiem, Caclutta: Gender and the Politics of Poverty.* Minneapolis: University of Minnesota Press. 2003. p. 1.

2   Standing, G. *The Precariat. The New Dangerous Class.* London and New York: Bloomsbury Academic. 2011.

3   Sassen, S. "Global Inter-city networks and Commodity Chains: Any Intersections?" In: *Global Networks.* 10(1). 2010. p. 152.

4   Ekers, M.Hamel, P.Keil, R. "Governing Suburbia: Modalities and Mechanism of Suburban Governance." In: Regional Studies. 46(3). 2012. p. 405–422.

5   For valuable studies of the historical origins of suburbs in preindustrial and colonial periods see Sjoberg, G (1960) *The Preindustrial City. Past and Present.* The Free Press: New York, 1960 and King. A.D. *The Bungalow: The Production of a Global Culture.* London: Routledge, 1984.

6   See Horne, D. *The Lucky Country.* Sydney: Penguin. 1960; and McGee, T. G./ McTaggart, W.D. "Petaling Jaya. A Socio-economic Survey of a New Town in Selangor, Malaysia." In: *Pacific Viewpoint Monograph No. 2.* 1967. Department of Geography, Victoria University of Wellington.

7   On "ethnoburbs" in France; for example, see Stebe, Jean-Marc, *La Crises Des Banlieues. Sociologie des Quartiers Sensible.* Paris: Presses Universitaires de France. 1999.
But perhaps the most influential writing has been Li, Wei. *Ethnoburb. The new Ethnic Community in Urban America.* University of Hawaii Press: Honolulu. 2009.
In New Zealand the Indian community I studied in the late 1950s was too small to develop as an ethnoburb but they still formed a social community that involved networks that were centered on the temple and community hall. (see McGee, T. G. "Indian Settlement in New Zealand, 1900–1956," In: *New Zealand Geographer.* 27(2). 1962. p. 203–233.

8   Freund P./ Martin, G. Driving South. The Globalization of Auto-Consumption and its Social Organization of Space. 1999. http://www.montclair.edu/hadish/drivessouthhtml. 14.09.04.

9   McGee, T.G./Erika de Castro (eds.): *Inclusion, Collaboration and Urban Government. Challenges in the Metropolitan Regions of Brazil and Canada.* Centre for Human Settlements. University of British Columbia. 2010.

10   McGee, T. G. "Malay Migration to Kuala Lumpur City: Individual Adaptation to the City." In: *Migration: Models and Adaptive Strategies.* Du Toit, B.M./Safa, H. (eds.): The Hague. Mouton Company. 1975. p. 143–78.

11   Davis, M. *Planet of Slums: Urban Involution and the Informal Working Class.* London: Verso, 2006.

12   See for example Harvey, D. *A Brief History of Neoliberalism.* Oxford: Oxford University Press. 2005 & Peck, J. *Constructions of Neoliberal Reason.* Oxford: Oxford University Press. 2010.
I have tried to deal with the concept of housing as a part of a consumption culture in McGee, T. G. "The Social Ecology of New Zealand Cities." In: *Social Process in New Zealand: Readings in Sociology.* Forster, J. (ed.): Auckland. 1969. p. 144–80 & McGee, T. G. "Mass Markets, Little Markets. Some Preliminary Thoughts on the Growth of Consumption and its Relationship to Urbanization: A Case Study of Malaysia." In: *Markets and Marketing* Plattner, S. (ed): Monographs in Economic Anthropology, No. 4. Washington, DC: University Press of America. 1985. p. 205–34 See also: Assadourian, E. "The Rise and Fall of Consumer Cultures. From Consumerism to Sustainability." In: *State of the World. 2010. Transforming Cultures. From Consumerism to Sustainability.* 2010. World Watch Institute. Washington: W.W. Norton. London and New York. p. 3–20.

13   Mc Gee, T.G. " Conservation and Dissolution in the Third World City. The Shantytown as an Element of Conservation" In: *Development and Change.* 10(1). 1979. p. 1–22.

GOVERNANCE AND GLOBAL SUBURBANISMS

Pierre Hamel

The urban century has produced myriad forms of global suburbanisms. Individual and public choices made by city builders and dwellers globally affect the way suburbs are built, maintained, governed, contested, and regulated. This poses the question of suburban governance. Suburban governance in the study of contemporary cities deserves our attention because with the production of global suburban spaces new theoretical and empirical challenges are arising. Who are the main agents responsible for the shape and expansion of suburbs? What importance of history and context have as explaining factors? Can we talk of specific "suburban ways of life"?

Processes of suburban governance are part of an emerging "fast-forward urbanism."[1] Discarding the categories from which the city is usually represented, "fast-forward urbanism" is based upon the changing scale of city-making that is the metroburbia or city region. Looking at the city as "a laboratory, incubator, and starting point for all future action,"[2] "fast-forward urbanism" is bringing in together professionals and social actors for adapting to contextual contingency "when climate, economy, technology and culture are all undergoing unpredictable but inevitable transformations."[3] First, it relies on the necessity to recognize the importance of "everyday actors and practices" in defining the vitality of the city. DIY urbanism is certainly viable. Second, it introduces a definite break with seeing design — urban, architectural and landscape — from the outside and/or from the top down. Finally, it supports the emergence of a new creativity in conceiving and implementing landscape urbanism. It is therefore working with people and thinking in terms of in vivo practices as opposed to in vitro that prevails: "The in vivo argues that new forms of urbanity begin with learning how things work and why — not with the intent of expressing or fetishizing them, but in order to think about how else things might work."[4]

It is this image of a "fast-forward urbanism" that I have in mind when trying to capture in a nutshell the way global suburban spaces are produced nowadays. If such a depiction can be useful to apprehend the ongoing reshaping of city forms through their connections to peripheral growth, it leaves open the question of power, conflict, compromise, and regulation among stakeholders. This is what the concept of governance can help to understand better, despite its notorious ambiguity and conceptual limitations.

Global suburban spaces and the processes of governance involved in their reshaping are transforming cities from the outside in. If suburbs differ from central cities, and if peripheral growth occurs through different models of suburban development, we can speak of increasing *prevalence and diversity of qualitatively distinct "suburban ways of life"*. Global suburbanisms are part of city-making everywhere. In reference to urban politics, suburban governance can be defined as a mechanism of regulation in order to cope with issues of territorial integration at a metropolitan, city region, or mega-city region scale. Two aspects

Spaces of suburban governance: Vaughan City Hall (2012)
Source: Roger Keil

deserve consideration. First, suburban governance has to be understood in a general frame-work of governance restructuring that reorganizes and connects relationships of state, private sector and civil society actors. Second, in regards to social and political actors, the new challenges and dilemmas raised by suburban expansion need to be addressed.

The notion of governance denotes approaches to politics open to designing networks of cooperation for steering public matters. Often associated with a "change in the meaning of government,"[5] governance comes with important transformations in the functioning of the state due to the limitations of its resources and capacity for responding to social demands. Conversely, it is the increasing importance of private actors involved in the policy process that should be underlined. Changing relationships between state and society are certainly at stake, even though this does not mean that the role of the state is diminished. Its governing capacity has not diminished: "… even when governments choose to govern in alternative ways, the state remains the pivotal player in establishing and operating governance strategies and partnerships."[6] Often, however, governance of suburban spaces has included a rescaling of state functions and responsibilities locally, regionally, and beyond.[7]

Under the label of governance, state regulation is being redefined with the contribution of economic actors and, at times, social actors coming from civil society, especially activists of the community organizing tradition (or voluntary organizations), or both. These clarifications do not however solve the ambiguities that are accompanying the notion.[8] Often governance is used in normative, ideologically charged ways as in the well-known "good governance" used by the World Bank and the United Nations since the mid-1990s.[9] Often, in connection with normative political principles, the notion carries a neoliberal, if not a liberal vision of the state, favoring its privatization. It is this conception of governance that has been criticized by many researchers, emphasizing that its claims are misleading in regards to its capacity of producing "inclusive policy making."[10] Governance networks and arrangements tend to put aside power relations among actors, while cooperation between them is seen as a given. In fact, the nature of state power and the links it establishes with dominant capitalist interests are dissolving in the virtues associated with the normative pretensions of governance.[11]

Ambiguities and shortcomings notwithstanding, governance remains an important notion in an age of generalized suburbanization. "Fast-forward urbanism" makes the conditions under which urbanization now takes place more fluid. The transformations of the state — including the restructuring of relations between state and society — that are introducing new institutional arrangements for decision-making come with challenging circumstances that governance can help apprehend. For that matter, I would connect the idea of governance to the notion of experience as developed by John Dewey.[12]

The primacy Dewey gives to experiment in social life can be related both to his radical liberalism, and to the importance he attributes to participatory democracy for improving the auto-corrective capacity of democratic societies. For him, being a social actor able to take part in public debates through active participation, is what "experiment" allows us to achieve. The experimental logic defined by Dewey is one that opens up the capacity for individuals to transform themselves and their environment at the same time. Looking at governance from that angle can help substantiate the content of the notion.

With respect to suburban development, governance can contribute to explore the way suburbs are adapting to "fast forward urbanism" that is taking place at a global scale. Raising the question how to cope with the uncertainty global suburbanisms is introducing in shaping cities of the twenty-first century, governance and more specifically suburban governance deals with issues of scale or scaling.[13] Suburban governance however has been largely overlooked by urban studies[14] even though surveys considering the development of city regions necessarily cope with urban spatial expansion and are concerned by the role taken by suburbs on this occasion. In light of this concern, it should be recalled that differences prevailed in regards to cultural and political traditions. While in the United States regional governance — including suburban governance — is dedicated in priority to the coordination of cities and their border suburbs, in Europe a greater level of "assertiveness" is expressed by all local actors taking part in regional collective agency.[15] The current pattern of

Spaces of suburban govern-
ance: York Region Administrative
Centre, Newmarket (2012)
Source: Roger Keil

urbanization that supports the emergence of a "New Metropolis" — one that is polycentric and includes "varying sized urban centers, subcenters and satellites"[16] — is changing deeply the nature of urban development. In addition, the intensity and extension of suburban development involved in these patterns raised the issue of cooperation and decision-making. The increased participation of non-central populations in metropolitan affairs has put the inclusiveness of collective decision-making on the agenda of regional politics.

This question needs to be addressed while taking into account the way social, economic, and political actors are making decisions in local areas according to values that are influenced by the increasing prevalence of global suburbanisms. The diversity of suburbs is certainly not lesser than the one characterizing central cities. And to some extent, this can be explained by the type of suburban governance actors are relying upon. This phenomenon can be explored in relation to the three different modalities of suburbanization that one can find in the literature on urban studies: self-built, state-led, and private-led suburbanization.[17] Present in "different historical moments and spaces," I would add that these three modalities of suburban development need to be considered as "ideal types" that are necessarily contextual bringing to the fore the diversity of processes at play in different re-

Spaces of suburban governance: Markham Civic Centre
(2012)
Source: Roger Keil

gions of the world. These models have been considered recently by a team of scholars who revised the ways suburban governance was implemented in different countries.[18] Looking at the way suburban governance was being defined in the Global North as well as in the Global South, they underlined the contradictions and tensions that are prevailing between the diverse categories of actors taking part in shaping suburban development. This said, at what scale is it possible to regulate suburban development?

From a historical perspective, North American suburbs are the products of a complex set of factors including the diffusion of liberal social values, the availability of technological innovations, and the prevalence of market rationality over state control. Public investment in infrastructure as supported by the state was also required in addition to the existence of political models of regulating private-led development, without restricting the initiatives taken by contractors and private developers.

Looking back at the last sixty years of suburban expansion and its consequences in terms of spatial unequal development raises the question of collective choice and public decision-making with regards to suburbanism. As for other economic and social controversies, in liberal democracies urban spatial expansion is submitted to conflict of interests and power relations. So far, the problem of democratizing collective choices in reference to suburban governance remains an open question.

Beyond the multiplicity of scales, the dilemma of sharing the costs — economic, social, and environmental — of territorial expansion remains difficult to overcome. Everyone wants to benefit from the contribution of others while limiting his/her own expenses. The alleged cooperation posited by mainstream suburban governance discourse is unable to solve such dilemma. It nevertheless underlines that the solution cannot be expected exclusively from state decision taken in an authoritative way decided from above. Provided that economic actors along with voluntary organizations and representatives of different pressure groups, in cooperation with the different tiers of the state, are involved in shaping the future of suburban development, conflicts of interests are strong. It is not exclusively a matter of scale, even though suburban governance reminds that pertinent public decisions are not taken at an exclusive local or extremely decentralized level. The relevant scale is increasingly the city region or even the mega-city region.

The institutional arrangements that are favored by governance can indeed correspond to a "romantic" representation of democracy. But this image is not the exclusive one. Other more pragmatic accounts are also possible, especially if we connect with Dewey's model of democracy. In this sense, conflicts over values and interests are open to struggles and confrontations, while the position of dominant actors needs to be challenged in the name of democratizing principles. In conclusion, it is important to note that, in the context of a "fast-forward urbanism," while the relationship between public and private space is being revised, an active participation of citizens can be experienced or remains open if one recalls Dewey's perspective. In relation to the increased connectivity characterizing "fast-forward urbanism," the possibilities of collective action are being redefined. Even though the new urban structural conditions tend to favor more individualistic type of expression, new forms of cooperation between public and private actors remain inevitable. The governance of global suburban expansion can no longer escape the necessity to find common ground for addressing the conflicts between stakeholders.

Endnotes

1 Cuff, D/Sherman, R. "Introduction." In: Cuff, D./Sherman, R. (eds.): *Fast-Forward Urbanism Rethinking Architecture's Engagement with the City*. New York: Princeton Architectural Press. 2011. p. 10–33.
2 Ibid., p. 13.
3 Ibid., p. 24.
4 Ibid., p. 26.
5 Rhodes, R. A. W. "Waves of Governance." In: Levi-Faur, D. (ed.): *The Oxford Handbook of Governance*. Oxford: Oxford University Press. 2012. p. 33 .
6 Levi-Faur, D. "From 'Big Government' to 'Big Governance'?" In: Levi-Faur, D. (ed.): *The Oxford Handbook of Governance*. Oxford: Oxford University Press. 2012. p.12.
7 Macdonald, S./Keil, R. "The Ontario Greenbelt: Shifting the Scales of the Sustainability Fix?" In: *The Professional Geographer. 64(2)*. 2012. p. 1–21.
8 Pierre, J. "Introduction: Understanding Governance." In: Pierre, J. (ed): *Debating Governance. Authority, Steering and Democracy*. Oxford: Oxford University Press. 2000. p. 3.
9 Rothstein, B. "Good Governance." In: Levi-Faur, D. (ed.): *The Oxford Handbook of Governance*. Oxford: Oxford University Press. 2012. p. 149.

10 Davies, J. S. *Challenging Governance Theory. From Networks to Hegemony*. Bristol: The Policy Press. 2011. p. 2.
11 Offe, C. Governance: An 'Empty Signifier'?" In: *Constellations*. 2000. 16(4). p. 550–562.
12 Dewey, J. *The Public and its Problems*. Carbondale: University Press Drive. 1915.
13 Jonas, A. E. G. "Regulating Suburban Politics." In: Lauria, M. (ed.): *Reconstructing Urban Regime Theory. Regulating Politics in Global Economy*, Thousand Oaks: Sage. 1997. p. 206–229.
14 Hamel, P. /Keil, R. (eds.) *Suburban Governance: A Global View*. Toronto: University of Toronto Press. Forthcoming, 2013.
15 Boudreau, J.A.,.Hamel, P./Jouve, B./ Keil, R. "New State Spaces in Canada: Metropolitanization in Montreal and Toronto Compared." In: *Urban Geography*. 28 (1). 2009. p. 30–53.
16 Lang, R./Knox, P. K. "The New Metropolis: Rethinking Megalopolis." In: *Regional Studies*. 43(6). 2009. p.794.
17 Ekers, M./Hamel, P./Keil, R. "Governing Suburbia: Modalities and Mechanisms of Suburban Governance." In: *Regional Studies*. 46(3). 2012. p. 405–422.
18 Hamel/Keil, 2013. Op. cit.

HOW LAND MARKETS MAKE AND CHANGE SUBURBS

Richard Harris

In the summer of 2012, I sometimes drove my son to a hobby farm on the outskirts of Hamilton, Ontario. Setting out from our city neighborhood, built in the 1920s, we would soon pass into a swathe of postwar development — a succession of low-density subdivisions, fast-food outlets, and strip malls interrupted by a shopping center, a cluster of fresh developments sprouting sales billboards, coupled with a strip of car dealerships — before breaking into open country. Here, at a faster pace, we would flash past a junkyard, a riding stable, a field of corn, a small quarry, the turnoff to a regional airport, an old motel with cabins, a new motel, an orphaned townhouse development, a cemetery, more fields, a piggery, and gas station, turning down a sideroad with an irregular scattering of modest homes dating from the 1940s to the 2000s, before reaching our destination.

Versions of this transect could be repeated in any North American city, passing from older to newer suburbs and then into a periurban zone. Depending on the city's size, this might take from ten minutes to an hour or more, but it took twenty minutes from my city of half a million. This transect hints at the peculiar character of suburban land, at once transitional and transitory, and also how it has developed. Although some features are uniquely North American, others speak to patterns and processes that can be found around the world.

The transitional aspect of suburban land is obvious, with its intermediate levels of population density. To understand how it is transitory, however, we must make an effort: to see the city block as one-time urban fringe; to see the rash of homes on a rural sideroad as future urbanity. Suburban land does not just lie between the country and the city, but in the long view each parcel and tract itself undergoes that transition, begging us to view it historically.[1] Guiding that evolution, almost everywhere, is a land market. Not *the* market, because land markets vary greatly in character, never corresponding to an ideal. But a market, nonetheless, with private land tenure, negotiated prices, and government regulation. In these terms, suburban land is converted from rural to urban, allocated to users, and in time redeveloped. The operations are rarely visible, sales billboards being an exception, but it is restless markets that make and remake the suburbs.

Simplifying, the transition from rural to urban has three stages: the periurban, the suburban, and the ambiguously urban. In a mid-sized city of fairly conventional shape, like Hamilton, stages are expressed loosely in rings of development surrounding the urban center. That is why, following a long intellectual tradition, I speak the language of zones. Even in Hamilton, however, the pattern is complicated in several directions, while in larger or older cities suburban nodes and edge cities may change the picture considerably, so that some speak of postsuburbia.[2] Even then, however, patterns of age and density appear and, however they map onto the landscape, the three stages make themselves felt.[3] Each has its own peculiarities and market dynamics. In many ways, however, the first is the most important, and also the most variable from country to country.

The periurban zone is, as some like to say, liminal, neither this nor that, full of possibility.[4] It is neither rural nor urban. Physically, it contains as wide a range of land uses as is imaginable, and in no apparent order. Socially, it is diverse and disconnected. The world of the farmer, with its seed suppliers, equipment dealerships, and community centers, rarely intersects with that of the new resident, probably a commuter who works, shops, and socializes elsewhere. And when these worlds of locals and newcomers do intersect they often conflict. Nowhere are the stakes over land use higher, in both environmental and economic terms. The periurban zone is often vital to the city as a source of water, food, and building materials, while also a convenient place for waste disposal.[5] Financially, land used for homes, offices, factories, and stores is always worth far more than for agricultural purposes, often by a factor of twenty. Converted to urban use, it jumps in value. Who reaps that "development gain" is a vital question any society must address. The answer is not obvious. Some say it should go to the owners, whether the farmer who sells off individual parcels on rural sideroad, or the developer who acquires land cheaply ahead of urban growth, and later promotes a townhome tract. Others point out that owners do nothing to earn the increment in land value, which should instead go into public coffers. Most countries have devised a muddle of policies that amount to a compromise. In Canada, for example, businesses pay capital gains tax on the appreciation in land value, but homeowners do not. Property owners are allowed to reap development gains, but land use regulations limit use and hence value.

Indeed, quite recently, Ontario legislation defined a greenbelt that, surrounding Hamilton and the adjacent Greater Toronto Area, placed an agricultural region beyond the reach of urban development. Much of the periurban transect that I described above lies in that belt. The contrasting values of land under fields, homes, and motels is frozen, with no compensation to those owners who, in time, hoped for a development gain. With the rules variable and the stakes high, at the periurban fringe the politics of regulation can become heated.

In much of the developing world, this story is complicated because rural and urban land tenure differs.[6] Urban land is usually owned privately in ways that are recorded and easily exchanged. Rural land is often held communally, which prevents or inhibits its sale. Such land may encircle the city, as in many parts of sub-Saharan Africa, or take the form of dis-

tinctive villages, as in China. Either way, the periurban zone dynamically juxtaposes whole cultures, compelling them to negotiate new economic and political rules. Often, private tenure wins out; sometimes, as in China for the present, an uneasy truce develops. More complex still, many of those settling the periurban zone are not, as near Hamilton, city workers who have moved out, but rural-urban migrants who are seeking urban opportunity. They may bring assumptions about land that contradict the market mentality. Everywhere, then, but especially in the developing world, the periurban zone is full of complex possibility, conflict, and intrigue.

By comparison, once in place, the newly suburban zone seems placid. With minor national variations, the typical model in North America and Europe over the past half-century has been of large-scale suburban development, where subdivisions, shopping centers, and office parks appear almost overnight.[7] This pattern has been driven by lenders who favor safe, standardized investment packages.[8] Since the 1980s, encouraged by globalizing capital markets, this model has spread in the developing world. There, major cities now boast planned, gated communities, and many feature large, integrated new town projects at the urban fringe, such as Delhi's Gurgaon district. Such places are governed by private covenants as well as municipal regulations, which restrict what residents and businesses can do. Once in place, there is no immediate pressure for land use change, and their mode of governance often resists it.

Dar es Salaam, Tanzania,
across its suburbs (2008)
Source: Alan Mabin

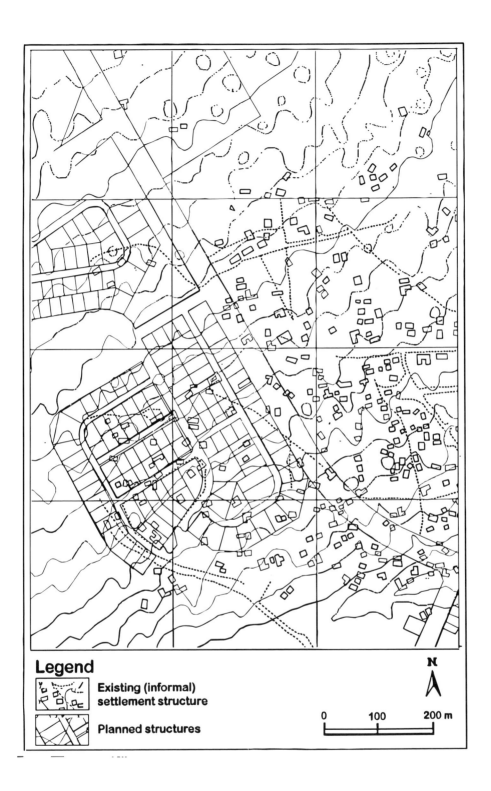

Legend

Existing (informal) settlement structure

Planned structures

N

| 0 | 100 | 200 m |

At the periurban fringe of cities in the Global South, informal and unplanned development is common. Rarely, develop- ers and/or municipalities replan these areas before they become fully built up suburbs. Chang'ombe, suburban Dar-es- Salaam, Tanzania (1987). Source: Kombe and Kreibich (2000).

Many suburbs, of course, were not produced all-at-once, and that is still true. Individual land parcels are developed piecemeal over a period of years, perhaps decades. Once the norm in North America — that is how my city neighborhood grew up — this is still common in Japan and even more so in the developing world.[9] There, many urban fringe areas are informally developed in an unplanned way that is sometimes corrected later, but usually not. Market forces squeeze out land-extensive uses, such as quarries, while newcomers lobby to expel the obnoxious, such as piggeries. But piecemeal areas are weakly regulated, so that some curious juxtapositions of the periurban phase persist.

Once the periurban zone has filled in and become suburban, inertia sets in for a while. Pressures for development, and with it the attention of developers, shift further outwards. Residents of the suburban zone grow attached to their neighborhoods, and if they own their homes they have a financial stake there too. The few attempts to modify building or redevelop sites are met with the familiar NIMBY (Not-in-my-Backyard) cry of resistance. The pace of change slows.

Change gathers pace again as suburbs age. If periurban growth continues, which it almost always does, once-young suburbs find themselves in an aging ring. Two trends create increasing pressures for redevelopment. Buildings age, deteriorate, and become anachronistic. At the same time, land that is becoming relatively more central — even if one of the relevant centers is itself suburban — becomes more valuable. The logic of redevelopment becomes compelling as new types of users, or old users with new tastes and needs, seek to move in. NIMBYism is still a brake, and so is the existing, often fragmented pattern of ownership. If an entrepreneur wants to redevelop an older suburban block, he must buy up all the land, and what happens if not everyone wants to sell? Governments have the power, variously labeled compulsory purchase or eminent domain, to enforce land assembly. But to exercise it, and face down opposition, they must believe that this is in the public interest, and that voters see it that way too.

Eventually, however, redevelopment happens, whether piecemeal or wholesale. This typically happens as the financial advantages become compelling: when the gap between current and potential land values reaches a critical, if ill-defined, threshold. On a modest scale, that is happening in my neighborhood now. A developer has replaced a café and parking lot with a six-story condominium, and is planning more condos on vacant sites nearby. It is fruitless to try to identify the moment when my block, and others like it, ceased to be suburban, or when a periurban district becomes solidly suburban. Indeed, to speak of zones at all is as much a matter of convenience as of reality. They are products of a continuous process, made up of innumerable events. By the time residents become aware that neighborhood-wide change has happened, it's history.

There's a lot about suburban development and redevelopment that we do not understand, so let me conclude by noting two especially important areas of ignorance. One of the most colorful characters in the suburban story are the developers of the quasi-legal, irregular settlements that surround many cities in the global south. Paradoxically, these settlements are tolerated, even encouraged, by the governments whose regulations they violate. The reasons are complex, and may involve bribery and vote-buying. To operate in such ambiguous settings, entrepreneurs and their syndicate allies must be financially shrewd and politically savvy. They are the unsung heroes and villains of the suburban fringe.

Although they shape whole subdivisions, informal developers are mere bit players in a larger, and even more obscure plot. Huge profits are made from suburban development, especially around rapidly growing cities. They attract big investors in a world of global capital flows. Some money goes into mere speculation, but massive amounts support useful investments in infrastructure. Suburban development, and the millions of people who benefit from it, is vulnerable to anything that stems or redirects such flows, including hiccups in the financial system. At the same time, property speculation has helped precipitate such crises, as it did during the Great Depression, in the Asian financial crisis of the 1990s, and the global meltdown of 2008. Making sense of how capital flows into, and out of, suburban property, and with what consequences, is the biggest and most important task of all.

Endnotes

1   McManus, R./Ethington, P. "Suburbs in Transition. New Approaches to Suburban History." In: *Urban History* 34(2). 2007. p. 317–337. Phelps, N./Wood,A.M./Valler, D.C. In "Post-Suburban World? An Outline of a Research Agenda. *Environment and Planning A.* 42(2). 2010. p. 366–383.

2   Ibid.

3   Angel, S. *Planet of Cities.* Cambridge, MA. Lincoln Institute of Land Policy. 2012.

4   Leaf, M. "Periurban Asia. A Commentary on 'Becoming Urban'". In: *Pacific Affairs.* 84(3). 2011. p. 525–534.
Simon, D. "Urban environments. Issues on the Peri-urban Fringe." In: *Annual Review of Environment and Resources 33.* 2008. p. 167–185.

5   Simon 2008, op. cit.

6   Dunkerley, H.B. (ed.): *Urban Land Policy. Issues and Opportunities.* New York: Oxford University Press. 1983.

7   Brown, H.J., Phillips, R.S., and Roberts, N.A. "Land Markets at the Urban Fringe." In: *Journal of the American Planning Association.* 47. 198. p. 131–144.

8   Leinberger, C. *The Option of Urbanism. Investing in a New American Dream.* Washington, DC: Island Press. 2009.

9   Sorensen, A. *The Making of Urban Japan: Cities and planning from Edo to the 21st Century.* London: Routledge. 2002.

THE INFRASTRUCTURE IS THE MESSAGE: SHAPING THE SUBURBAN MORPHOLOGY AND LIFESTYLE

Pierre Filion

"... the 'message' of any medium or technology is the change of scale or pace or pattern that it introduces into human affairs."

Marshall McLuhan, 1964[1]

As I borrow from Marshall McLuhan's perspective on the influence of media on society to conceptualize the effects of infrastructures on suburban form and lifestyle, it is logical to begin with a brief exploration of his thinking on media.

It is not as far-fetched as it may seem to rely on a conceptual framework devised to cast light on the impact of the media to further the understanding of infrastructures and their effect on urban morphology and human behavior. McLuhan's thinking was indeed deeply influenced by the historical model proposed by his University of Toronto colleague, economist Harold Innis, to explain how over centuries changes in European demand for Canadian staples shaped transportation systems between Canada and Europe and within Canada, and thereby determined the size and nature of settlement patterns and eventually the political institutions of this country.[2]

For McLuhan, it is not the content of the messages transported by the different media that is most influential, but the very characteristics of the media themselves. In his perspective, these features fashion messages in the image of each media. For example, the profound influence the television has had on society was primarily a function of how it conveys information (certain messages are compatible with television others are not) as well as of the changes it brought in how people think and organize their lives. Hence the aphorism "the medium is the message."[3]

I take the view in this chapter that just as the impact of media on society stems from their general nature rather than the content of their messages, infrastructures play a role in shaping the suburb that extends well beyond their specific functions. Infrastructures can be seen as the media and their message as the form suburban development takes. In other words, the contribution of infrastructures is not limited to their assigned task of conveying flows. Accordingly, transportation and sewage networks do not only carry people and goods or evacuate human waste; they also have a determining effect on the location and form of urban development, especially on its density. The same goes for other infrastructures: water distribution, electricity, and electronic transmission, for example. And the step from suburban morphology to lifestyle is an easy one to make. Time budgets and work and consumption behavior are tributary of the nature of activities present in suburbs and their distribution. So, as infrastructures are a major factor in the shape taken by suburban development, they de facto contribute to the suburban lifestyle.

The post Second World War North American suburb heralded a new urban form, marking a radical break from prior development patterns. The novelty of the suburban environment is made plain when contrasted with previous forms of urban development. Before the war, North American cities were relatively compact, featuring mixed land use and a centralized configuration focused on the central business district. The prewar urban morphology mirrored limitations in the reach of infrastructure networks, which meant that serviced land was at a premium. New developments had to locate where the roads, pipes and wires were available, and close to public transit routes (mostly streetcars until the 1930s). The form of cities was also shaped by the centralizing and clustering tendencies inherent in the infrastructure systems of the time.

For example, reliance on coal power for steam generation encouraged industrial employment to congregate in large, generally multistory buildings, across which motion generated by heavy and expensive steam engines could be distributed to activate machines. Moreover, these structures had to locate where coal could conveniently be delivered. The two main urban modes of transportation before the generalization of car use — walking for close-by journeys and public transit for longer trips — made a major contribution to the form of cities. These journey patterns account for the presence of stores close to or within residential areas, typically in a main street configuration, for walking was how local retailing was accessed. And the radial nature of public transit networks accounts for the usual absence of substantial intermediary centers between the large downtown concentration of activities and local commercial streets. A strong reliance on public transit thus went hand-in-hand with the highly centralized nature of prewar cities.

A cursory look at aerial photographs is sufficient to reveal the stark difference between pre- and postwar urban development. After the war, the consumption of space increased dramatically, the road network was transformed by wide arterials organized in a super-grid configuration and curvilinear road layouts within super-blocks, expressways crisscrossed metropolitan regions, and multi-functionality waned as land use specialized. Above all, cities went rapidly from being highly centralized to taking on a dispersed pattern whereby structuring activities (employment, retailing, institutions) scattered at various points of high automobile accessibility and thus became separated from each other.[4] Suburban features that catch the eye when looking from above are the abundance of green space, the large amount of land given to the car and functional specialization.

What is the relation between infrastructures and the postwar suburban form? There was first the effect of the infrastructure boom of the postwar decades, driven by a prosperous economy and flush government coffers. Infrastructure development was propelled by senior and local governments. The federal government in the US and federal and provincial administrations in Canada contributed large sums towards the creation of expressway networks in metropolitan regions. Meanwhile, suburban municipalities, competing against each other to lure development, were quick to invest in other forms of infrastructure.[5] The resulting large supply of infrastructures made it possible for the postwar suburb to dramatically increase land consumption standards, while the nature of postwar urban infrastructures encouraged decentralization.[6]

Four-level freeway interchange,
Los Angeles (2012)
Source: Roger Keil

For example, growing reliance on electricity in manufacturing made the relocation of production to suburban industrial parks possible. Of course, rising car use also played a key role in the decentralization of manufacturing as it did in that of all other activities. Communication technologies also contributed to the suburban form and lifestyle. One characteristic of the suburban landscape is the predominance of single-family homes and a significant expansion in the size of residential units. Associated with this phenomenon is the tendency to internalize within the suburban home many activities that used to take place outside the home, at the expense of cinemas, theatres, café, and street life in general. The television, home theaters and the Internet have contributed to in-house entertainment, and information technology makes it possible for a growing number of people to work from home at least some of the time. In a sense, this tendency can be seen as the ultimate decentralization of urban activities, down to the level of the house.

Infrastructures indeed appear to have played a key role in the definition of the postwar suburban form and, consequentially, of its lifestyle. To paraphrase McLuhan, infrastructures are the suburb. Yet one has to acknowledge that infrastructures were not alone in defining the suburban form. Regulations also played a role. The rigid functional specialization of suburban land indeed rests on the enforcement of zoning. But as zoning often serves to maximize the development potential, and thus the fiscal yield, of land parcels, it tends to coincide with market preferences as influenced by the presence and nature of infrastructures. In these

Layered suburban infrastructure,
San Fernando Road,
Los Angeles (2012)
Source: Roger Keil

circumstances, development guided by zoning is not all that different from instances where zoning is absent, as in Houston. There is also the fact that zoning can be modified more easily than existing infrastructures.

The perspective developed in the chapter has important implications for the relation between infrastructures, suburban form and lifestyle in the present difficult economic climate. If infrastructures shaped the suburb, what happens when the liberal funding required for the building and maintaining of the level of infrastructures associated with the dispersed suburban form is no longer available? North American suburbs, over their development phase, have typically enjoyed easy access to infrastructure funding via senior governments or by issuing municipal bonds or levying development charges. The surfeit of suburban infrastructures is not surprising given these favorable financial circumstances. But the financial landscape of suburbs is changing, making it difficult for many municipal administrations to provide and maintain levels of infrastructures required to sustain the dispersed suburb.

There are first the problems encountered by maturing suburban municipalities. With no developable land left, increasing de-industrialization as some of their production units reach the end of their lifecycles, and an overall depreciation of their aging built environment, these suburban administrations lack the revenue streams needed to maintain and update their infrastructure. To make things worse, the filtering down of the housing stock leads to the arrival of a population which is more dependent on municipal services, such as public transit. Other financial problems are caused by recessions. For example, rapidly developing US suburban municipalities have borrowed large sums to provide infrastructure for new developments over the 2000s, which have lost much of their market value with the onset of

Palmdale: Water and wind
energy in California's desert
suburbs (2012)
Source: Roger Keil

the Great Recession. Unable to service bonds with tax revenues from these developments, some of which deserve the label of "ghost estates," many municipalities teeter on the brink of bankruptcy despite having severely curtailed their services.[7] There is finally the troubling coincidence between an eroding public sector funding capacity and the disproportional inflation affecting infrastructure construction and maintenance. While outsourcing and greater efficiency in the production of goods pushes down inflation levels, sectors of the economy where productivity gains are limited, such as construction, have the opposite effect. Such a situation creates a quandary for public sector agencies: as the limited sums at their disposal reflect current low rates of economic growth and inflation, their capacity to fund inflating infrastructures is curtailed.

What happens to suburbs when the construction and maintenance of the infrastructures responsible for their dispersed form are cut back, when the quantity and quality of infrastructures is depleted? Will we confront a situation where "what infrastructure giveth, infrastructure taketh away," resulting in a deterioration and decline of the dispersed suburb translating in falling quality of life and property values? Or will a new suburban form, adapted to reduced infrastructures and possibly changing values, such as environmental awareness, emerge from these difficulties? While it is too early to answer these questions, it is undeniable that the North American suburb will need to find ways to adapt to profound changes in financial circumstances.

Intermodal Drive, Brampton,
Ontario (2012)
Source: Roger Keil

Admittedly, the North American postwar model provides an extreme depiction of the relation between suburban morphology and the extent and nature of infrastructures. Nowhere has overall infrastructure development been as extensive and transportation networks as narrowly centered on a single mode. As a result, not only do the resulting suburban form and lifestyle hit a financial wall in some instances, but they also come out as extreme when compared to international suburban models. At the risk of gross oversimplification, I introduce briefly two global versions of the suburb: the mixed suburb and the deprived suburb.

Mixed suburbs are found in parts of the world which, while enjoying well-developed infrastructure systems, have not experienced the lavish outlay on infrastructures characteristic of the North American postwar suburb and largely responsible for its low density and the ample space it consumes. The nature of infrastructures also distinguishes mixed suburbs from their North American counterparts. Although the car undeniably plays an important role in mixed suburbs, these sectors also benefit from the presence of quality public transportation. Their texture reflects this dual transportation system; mixed suburbs combine low-density, functionally specialized environments, which are heavily reliant on cars, with transit-oriented configurations featuring higher density and multifunctionality.

Obviously, other factors than infrastructures also explain differences in suburban form. Regulations, especially those that set urban growth boundaries, play a role as does the value of rural relative to urban land. Mixed suburbs are most prevalent in Europe and in developed and developing Asian countries.[8]

In the other suburban model, the deprived suburb, formal infrastructure networks are minimal and needs are largely met through self-reliance efforts. As they are not structured by planned infrastructure networks, these settlements develop in a haphazard fashion, guided mostly by uncoordinated infrastructures produced by the informal sector. In this case, it is not primarily infrastructures that determine the location and form of suburban developments, as the land available (legally or illegally) for such developments plays a part that is as, if not more, important. Scarce infrastructures and land account for a large proportion of space taken by the footprint of buildings.[9] The density of these suburbs is, however, limited by informal building processes' incapacity to erect high-rise buildings.

Endnotes

1 McLuhan, M. *Understanding Media: The Extensions of Man.* Cambridge: MIT Press. 1994. [1964] p. 8.

2 Innis, H. A. *The Fur Trade in Canada: An Introduction to Canadian Economic History.* Toronto: University of Toronto Press. 1956.

3 McLuhan, M./Fiore, Q. *The Medium Is the Massage: An Inventory of Effects.* New York: Random House. 1967.

4 Lewis, P. F. "The Galactic Metropolis." In Platt, R. H./Macinko, G. (eds.) *Beyond the Urban Fringe.* Minneapolis, MN. 1983. p. 23–49.

5 Hayden, D. "Building the American Way: Public Subsidy, Private Space." In: Nicolaides, B.M./Wiese, A. (eds.): *The Suburb Reader.* New York: Routledge. 2006. p. 273–280.

6 Speir, C./ Stephenson, K. "Does Sprawl Cost us All? Isolating the Effects of Housing Patterns on Public Water and Sewer Costs." *Journal of the American Planning Association.* 2002. 68. p. 56–71.

7 Wasik, J. F. "In Uncertain Times, Municipal Bonds Call for Caution." In *New York Times* (Oct. 19, 2011) p. 2.

8 Jenks, M./Burgess, R. (eds.): *Compact Cities: Sustainable Urban Forms for Developing Countries.* London: Spon Press. 2000.

9 Neuwirth, R. *Shadow Cities: A Billion Squatters, a New Urban World.* New York: Routledge. 2005.

WE'RE A LONG WAY FROM LEVITTOWN, DOROTHY: EVERYDAY SUBURBANISM AS A GLOBAL WAY OF LIFE

Lisa Drummond &
Danielle Labbé

"[T]he ultimate effect of the suburban escape in our time is, ironically, a low-grade uniform environment from which escape is impossible."   Lewis Mumford, 1961[1]

"[W]e might say that all suburbs are urbanizing from the moment they are built."
Tineke Lupi and Sapo Muster, 2006[2]

"[U]nplanned suburban development is not the only process of urban development one observes in the Global South."   Mark Clapson and Ray Hutchison, 2010[3]

"[T]oday's 'suburbia' might be as restless, even chaotic a concept as the urban frontier itself."
Kay Anderson, 2006[4]

When Herbert Gans undertook his landmark study of Levittown, USA in 1958, the prevailing view of urban social life was of an existence spent lost in an anonymous urban crowd, with few meaningful daily interactions, and a disappearing sense of neighborhood, community, or even family as providing social bonds of any significance (*contra* Wirth, Simmel). Gans's study of the middle-class suburbanites in the new settlement of Levittown[5] upended that view. For him, neighborliness emerged to fill the social vacuum created by the weakening of kinship ties in the city, and the Levittowners he documented enjoyed lives of rich sociability and local engagement with place.

Half a century later, the forms of settlement that might be included in a contemporary inventory of "suburbs" range far beyond that Anglo-American Levittown of identikit houses or the endless array of backyard pools that made Burt Lancaster's journey by water across suburban Connecticut possible (in *The Swimmer*, 1968). Today's global expressions of suburban place include those familiar images, but also erstwhile rural settlements experiencing *in situ* urbanization or being engulfed into expanding urban fabrics, gated communities, and other exclusive residential estates built at the urban periphery, along with the more informal periurban places variously labeled slums — shantytowns, *favelas, bidonvilles, kampongs, barrios*, etc. Suburbanites of the global north and south include all manner of social, economic, and cultural forms: from a gun-toting, hoodie-abhorring resident of a wealthy gated community in Florida, USA; to a real estate agent renting out two-story villas in the *favelas* of Rio de Janeiro, Brazil; to an upland-residing ethnic minority group member marooned within the new borders of the national capital of Hanoi, Vietnam.

Even in the US, the idea of suburbia can no longer be contained within an image of precisely manicured lawns or New Urbanist-style front porches. Scholarship on suburbs in the US demonstrates that in many places, peripheral neighborhoods have turned into cosmopolitan worlds, forged by second- and third-generation internal and international migrants.[6] Suburbs are, moreover, increasingly home to socioeconomic disparities between the poor, middle, and the more affluent segments of populations on the fringe,[7] and to highly differentiated family and household compositions, along with mixed male and female labor forces that blur conceptions of "feminized" suburbs versus a "masculinized" city.[8]

Is there even enough at the core of the concept and practice of "suburban living" to warrant a notion of "everyday suburbanisms"? Such concern prompted Kay Anderson to ask: "Is twenty-first-century suburbanism a mode of city living with its own set of defining cultural and landscape values? ... Was this human habitus ever so fixed a set of attributes and experiences?"[9]

It is worth considering the question seriously, though at the same time, the "mythic thinking about suburban places"[10] is sufficiently deeply rooted that confronting the mythology head-on seems a more immediate and productive route.

Suburbs are, at least in the Anglo-American model, still commonly represented as "nonplaces": vast developments of largely identical housing types and residents where private

life takes priority over public life.[11] Suburbanites are seen as being more and more socially isolated and, for this reason, have been deemed, by various social commentators, to threaten the stability of the broader society to which they belong.[12] This perspective on suburban community life has been labeled the "Lost View."[13]

Beyond the globalized suburban form of gated communities and the Lost-View-inspired questions of sociospatial exclusion, privatization, and fragmentation that it provokes,[14] other forms of suburbs have been largely subsumed under the negative image of the "spontaneous" or informal periurban settlement regardless of which label from the list above they are given (*favela, barrio, kampong*, etc.) or their various geographical, social, and cultural locations. Despite the fact that these various peripheral settlements of the developing world can be dynamic places that productively bring newcomers into the urban sphere, they continue to be defined, in the language of urban planners and governments, as static, marginal spaces of inexpensive dwellings containing poor people, usually in less than salubrious conditions; frequently considered cancerous growths on an otherwise healthy city.[15]

The Manor, Hanoi: a suburban residential development for the wealthy tries to offer a European street experience (2011)

Source: Lisa Drummond

The Lost View and other dystopian clichés of suburbia (or even utopian clichés, for that matter) do, of course, have real, on-the-ground implications. Popular media depictions of suburban forms and ways of life do affect suburbanites' view of themselves, their everyday practices, and their interactions with the rest of the city, as well as outsiders' views, practices, and often, importantly, policies and plans. The labels themselves, in fact, are often telling in terms of the meanings associated with the spaces they describe, their non-central location (*barrio*), an original peripheral location of a slum settlement (*favela*), the unofficial and un-regulated nature of their establishment (*'ashwa 'iyyat*), or their supposed rural and therefore backward character (*kampong*).

In the *'ashwa'iyyat* (literally, "haphazard") of Cairo, for example, Ismail argues that the label itself connoted "what went wrong with the city." The residents understood that they were stigmatized by the rest of the city because of their location in the 'ashwa'iyyat, but at the same time were themselves critical of residents of other urban areas and of other urban lifestyles.[16]

In a rare longitudinal study, which revisited Rio's favelas in the early 2000s after an original study in 1969, Janice Perlman found that while favelas are, in most respects, now well integrated into the city, their residents continue to suffer from severe, place-based, social stigmatization. She writes: "The only remaining distinction between favelas (often called *morros* or hills) and the rest of the city (commonly referred to as the *asfalto* or pavement) is the deeply-rooted stigma that still adheres to them."[17]

Suburban high-rise project under
construction on the outskirts of
Hanoi (2012)
Source: Danielle Labbé

She adds that, today, living in a favela is the most powerful dimension of social exclusion faced by the city's poor, "more prejudicial than being dark-skinned, poorly dressed, a migrant, or female."[18]

"Spontaneous" or "informal" settlements, are, of course, not the only suburban form to be found outside North America and Europe. Gated communities are often, for societies of the global South, important spaces in which ideas of what is and how to be middle class are played out, as well as, of course, being in their most luxurious forms, spaces for the elite.[19] Those gated communities, moreover, must be understood as not simply a clone of the North American model. In a study of gated communities in Shanghai, for example, Pow Choon-Piew argued that the exclusivity of such spaces understood in their local context could be seen as offering not isolation and withdrawal from social life, à la the US model of such suburbs, but spaces of "greater household autonomy and personal freedom" precisely because they work to "keep out" the Chinese Communist state — metaphorically and sometimes even literally, with Party officials stopped at the gates — while at the same time allowing residents increased global connectivity via satellite TV, which is elsewhere banned in private homes.[20]

The curse of the so-called Anglo-American model of suburbs, in particular its myths and clichés, is that it prevents a more nuanced understanding of everyday suburban experience in the global South and Global North. As the urban-suburban divide is progressively blurred,

Suburban housing under
construction on the ouskirts of
Hanoi (2012)
Source: Danielle Labbé

and as suburbanites are increasingly faced with myriad transformations affecting their living environment and communities, understanding the practice of suburban life requires attentiveness to the new suburban processes in the global South in particular that might or might not reproduce established patterns in countries that suburbanized earlier. Across the global south, cities are experiencing the construction, on outer urban edges, of informal periurban areas, new commercial developments, industrial compounds, and middle-class housing estates which often sit cheek-by-jowl. Our studies of suburban everyday life, in other words, will require attention to the practices and the spaces of social interaction across the spectrum of suburban places and forms.

Endnotes

1 Mumford, L. *The City in History: Its Origins, its Transformations, and its Prospects*. New York: Harcourt, Brace and World. 1961.

2 Lupi, T./Muster, S. "The Suburban 'Community Question.'" In: *Urban Studies. 43(4)*. 2006. p. 801–17.

3 Clapson, M./Hutchison, R. "Introduction: Suburbanization in Global Society." In: *Suburbanization in Global Society. Clapson, M./Hutchison, R. (eds.): Bingley. Emerald Group*. 2010. p. 1–14.

4 Anderson, K. "Introduction: After Sprawl: Post-Suburban Sydney." In: *Post-Suburban Sydney: The City in Transformation*. Sydney. 2006.

5 Wirth, L. "Urbanism as a Way of Life." In: *American Journal of Sociology. 44(1)*. 1938. p. 1-24.
& Simmel, G. "The Metropolis and Mental Life." In: Kasinitz, P. (ed.): *Metropolis: Centre and Symbol of our Times*. New York: New York University Press. 1995 [1903, 1971]. p. 30–35.
Gans, H. J. *The Levittowners: How People Live and Politic in Suburbia*. New York: Pantheon Books. 1967.

6 Saunders, D. *Arrival City: How the Largest Migration in History is Reshaping our World*. London: William Heinemann. 2010. p. 95.
"As of 2005, for the first time more immigrants were living in the suburbs than in the central cities of the United States, with immigrants settling in the burbs outnumbering downtown arrivals by almost two to one. This trend has transformed the suburbs. Racial and ethnic minorities now represent a third of the population of America's suburbs, up from 19 percent in 1990."
See Also: Li, W. *Ethnoburb: The New Ethnic Community in Urban America*. Honolulu: University of Hawaii Press. 2009.

7 Murphy, A. K. "The Suburban Ghetto: The Legacy of Herbert Gans in Understanding the Experience of Poverty in Recently Impoverished American Suburbs." In: *City and Community. 6(1)*. 2007. p. 21–137

8 Anderson, 2006. Op. cit.

9 Ibid., p. 4.

10 McDonogh, G. W. "Suburban Place, Mythic Thinking, and the Transformations of Global Cities." In: *Urban Anthropology and Studies of Cultural Systems and World Economic Development*. 2006. 35(4). p. 471–501.

11 Oldrup, H. H. "Suburban socialities: Between everyday life and urban leisure space in the metropolitan region." In *Home Cultures*. 2009. 6(3): 311–32.
See also: Murphy, 2007 Op. Cit. p. 23.
& Baldassare, M. "Suburban Communities." In: *Annual Review of Sociology. 18*. 1992. p. 476.

12 For example:
Putnam, R. D. *Bowling Alone. The Collapse and Revival of American Community*. New York: Touchstone. 2000. Chapter 2.

13 Lupi/Muster, 2006. Op. Cit.

14 For example: Dick, H. W./Rimmer, P.J. "Beyond the Third World City: The New Urban Geography of South-East Asia." In: *Urban Studies. 1998*. 35(12). p. 2302–21.
& Leisch, H. "Gated Communities in Indonesia." *Cities. 19(5). 2002*. p. 341–50.

15 Ismail, S. *Political Life in Cairo's New Quarters: Encountering the Everyday State. Minneapolis: University of Minnesota Press. 2006*.

16 Ibid. p. 18.

17 Perlman, J. E. *Favela: Four Decades of Living on the Edge of Rio de Janeiro*. Oxford: Oxford University Press. 2007. p.10.

18 Ibid. p. 24.

19 Genis, S. "Producing elite localities: the rise of gated communities in Istanbul." In: *Urban Studies. 2007*. 44. p. 771–98.
See also: Clapson/Hutchison, 2010. Op. Cit. and Leisch, 2002. Op. Cit.

20 Choon-Piew, P. *Gated Communities in China: Class, Privilege and the Moral Politics of the Good Life*. London: Routledge. 2009. pp. 83, 94, 96.

HIKING THE MEXICO PERIPHERY

Feike De Jong

Despite the poor pedestrian infrastructure, these pedestrian paths are
built independent of roads in informal neighborhoods and are successful in generating pedestrian activity.

These patterns of dirt roads seen at the edge of the Greater Mexico
City area lack sidewalks or drainage because they are built for
short term convenience. They are hard to change when neighborhoods around them start to consolidate.

Settlement patterns tend toward leaving the edge of
the megalopolis relatively clear because of the impact
of physical obstacles to the growth of the city such as
these hills on urban morphology. Settlement tends to
cluster on the edge of the agglomeration due to their
nearness to existing infrastructure and the difficulty
of negotiating new infrastructure with authorities.

The Limitropias project by journalist Feike de Jong is an effort to document and understand the precise edge of the Greater Mexico City Area. Underlying this effort is the desire to understand the processes behind the conversion of the countryside into city.

2

THEMES

FLEXSPACE – SUBURBAN FORMS

Ute Lehrer

From the early settlements which were a manifestation of concentrated human activities in space to the modern period, the form of cities has defined our imagination.[1] Constantly evolving, reflecting technological changes, such as the invention of steel, the form of the city has undergone major changes within the past two hundred years. In the twentieth century, most of the industrial cities in the West have replaced their smokestacks with office towers. Similarly, we have witnessed a profound shift in residential housing from the nineteenth century onward, with a move outwards into the peripheries of urbanized areas. While the dominant notion of the contemporary Western city remains the image of a dense downtown with high-rise towers surrounded by residential zones, the real existing spatial form of cities has changed. New urban forms are developing at the fringe, the periphery, the liminal space at the border of city and suburb, and between urbanized areas and the space "out–there." This is where the interesting sociospatial manifestations of an urbanized society are showing their face.

It is also here, where the dominant images that were produced in the Global North are clashing with the reality of most cities around the world. Therefore we can postulate that the cities we encounter today are no longer explained through the language that has dominated urban studies over the last hundred years, in which cities were seen as closed and identifiable units in a Weberian sense, combined with the modern metropolis perspective based on a gravitational model, as described by the Chicago School. The latter's concentric model was outlived by the 1980s, when economic restructuring and flexible production systems left their imprint on the urban fabric of most cities. Cities of today look much more amorphous. They are complex spaces that no longer can be read from the inside

out and are perhaps, closer to what urban centers looked like in the early days of human settlements.

Spiro Kostof, in his ground-breaking work on form, structures, and ruptures, reminds us that early urban forms came in different articulations — from arbitrary irregularities due to the amalgamation of various villages into city-states, to intentionally designed cities with artificial layout and geometric purity; from service areas that developed next to sites of power and wealth, to the total replacement of old structures by erecting entirely new cities in their place. He also discussed the role of temples, palaces, and other forms of monuments within the center of human settlement as well as on the outskirts. His description of earlier cities as oscillating between rigid forms and uneven spatial pattern can be applied to the form of today's cities.[2]

The urban forms of today's cities are multifarious, particularly on the outskirts where different users and usages are juxtaposed. The shiny façades of office parks meet agricultural lands; highly connected places are next-door neighbors to areas that are cut off from the urban region; advanced infrastructure can be found adjacent to service deserts; high-rise towers greet single family homes; large driveways and swimming pools are on the other side of the fence from industrial sites; large-scale shopping malls and multiplex cinemas are encroaching into ravines and natural landscapes; production and consumption form this new urban space as much as they form spaces of neglect and abandonment or the hyper-planned and manicured landscape.

It is the periphery that underwent significant changes during the past thirty years: no longer is it only a site for bedroom communities with their monotonous land use patterns,

FlexSpace: Vineyards, high-tech service establishments and shopping mix along an arterial road outside Montpellier, France (2009)
Source: Roger Keil

but it has evolved into an urban form for which we still are lacking a distinct vocabulary: Technoburb,[3] Edge City,[4] FlexSpace,[5] Boomburbs,[6] and Metroburbia[7] are terms that have the impetus to force us to rethink our notion of what is happening on the outskirts of many cities. Besides servicing the continuous expansion of single-family houses, they have become sites for office functions, retail, and other usages that historically were situated in the city center. This urban landscape, found both between the city and the suburb and on the outer fringes, is defined by large infrastructure elements such as electricity lines, freeways, and railways. Local public transport is often lacking and individual mobility is based around the car. In the North American context, the division of land into so-called super-grids is a defining feature. Within these grids functions are segregated from each other leading to insulated land uses.[8]

While spatial pattern and land use categories drew the attention of urban scholars throughout the twentieth century,[9] there has been a plethora of different attempts to describe the structural changes that have arisen since the 1980s.[10] Geographers linked urban form with economic restructuring and the productive forces that led to new spatial articulations.[11] In the early 1990s, Edward Soja coined the term "Exopolis, the city without" to explain the new spatial configurations that he identified as a result of the dynamics of dispersion and decentralization with simultaneous reconcentration.[12] At the same time, sociologist Sharon Zukin called the city a "matrix of capital accumulation"[13] identifying two simultaneous processes: a reconcentration of production and transportation and the production of the suburban landscape as "small-scale outcroppings in the hinterland of shopping malls, ranch houses, and office parks."[14] And in an attempt to counter the dominant perspective of the gravitational model, Dear and Flusty argued that today's cities look much more like checkerboards than concentric circles. They called their model of a centerless urban form "Keno capitalism," meaning that the logic of investing in a geographical space no longer has to do with what can be found in its proximity and that the periphery reorganizes the center through a reterritorialization of the urban process, resulting in ubiquitous social polarization.[15]

Most of the focus on new urban forms in the periphery is driven by the North American experience of a visible downtown and its ubiquitous low-rise and formulaic outward growth. However, European cities, with their suburban expansions into the countryside, are not far behind. In the early 1990s, a similar phenomenon was described in the case of Switzerland and to a certain degree for Frankfurt.[16] In France and Italy, cities have developed tentacle-like hybrid commercial zones, expanding along transport arteries, reaching out into the agricultural landscapes. The spatial articulation of the decentralization forces of the compact European city led Thomas Sieverts to argue that the new forms are hybrid; they are landscaped cities or urbanized landscapes, and he called these spaces *Zwischenstadt*, or in English, "In-between-city." It is the area that is wedged between the old city and the open countryside, between living places and non-places of mobility, connected to the global mar-

ket flows while at the same time part of local economic cycles. Developed within a specific German context, this way of reading new urban forms has been adapted for the North American context in order to describe areas that can be found between the city and the suburbs.[17] Of particular significance is the division of land into "areas of aggressive expansion" and areas that enjoy "little attention from the cities' investors and resident communities … As a consequence, infrastructure built to connect centers actually disconnect those non-central spaces that lie in-between," creating new physical as well as socioeconomic imbalance on the periphery by dissecting these residual spaces with thruways and bypasses.[18]

The motivation to build at the edge of the city is twofold. On the one hand, there is the regulated and strategic growth that is instigated by the political elites of the urban center. It takes advantage of the relatively unproblematic availability of land compared to the inner city, where any new construction needs to negotiate with various owners and usages. At the edge of cities, we usually find land that has little if any construction on it, and the land ownership is not as fine grained. This is where cities of the Global South and North express similar dynamics: large-scale projects such as airports, garbage dumps, universities, distribution centers, hospitals, and power stations are put to the edge of the city. This is the dynamic to have "stuff" outside of the city, the things that are necessary but that are not welcome within the center of the city. On the other hand, there is continued settlement in the periphery that is fueled by immigration. Here the Global South and North might

Shiny facades of office buildings are popping up arbitrarily throughout the former agricultural landscape, together with freeways, retail spaces, and housing (2009).
Source: Ute Lehrer

look different at first sight, with informal settlement as a dominant form for the former and developer-driven, cookie-cutter subdivision for the latter — usually initiated by place-based interests. Within the areas of informality, there is a greater possibility to remake the urban,[19] though also in the areas of formalized fuzziness there is great potential for a strong urban articulation. What these two areas share in common is the belief that the proximity to the city will provide the economic and physical platform for a better life.[20]

Both of these dynamics for developing land at the edge of the city leave us with urban forms that are difficult to read. We can find clearly defined edges next to fuzzy areas that don't seem to start or to end, and that don't seem to have any centers.[21] Some areas have a high degree of flexibility, both in terms of users and usages. What we also find are the connectors between these areas and urban centers, roads that are also the location of service and retail facilities,[22] while at the same time, these areas are often dissected by super-highways, allowing connectivity only to certain sections while leaving out entire others. These spatial articulations of new urban forms, with their hybridity and irregularity bring us back to what Kostof already had identified for some early human settlements. Undoubtedly, the structural and technological differences between then and now are significant, but it is striking how the spatial articulations of new urban forms follow a logic of order and chaos, regulation and informality, nodal points and neglect areas, all very similar to what was described for the historical city. In regard to these spaces, we still need to develop ways of seeing, a proper language that goes with it, and an analysis that takes into account the various factors that shape these spaces, from infrastructure, to regulations, to human agency, and to everyday life practices.

Endnotes

1 Kostof. S. *The City Shaped: Urban Patterns and Meanings Through History*. London: Thames and Hudson. London. 1991.
2 Ibid., p. 34–36.
3 Fishman, R. *Bourgeois Utopias: The Rise and Fall of Suburbia*. New York: Basic Books: 1987.
4 Garreau, J. *Edge City: Life on the New Frontier*. New York: Doubleday. 1991.
5 Lehrer, U. "The Image of the Periphery: The Architecture of Flex-Space." In: *Environment and Planning D: Society and Space*. 1994. 12 (2). p. 187–205.
6 Lang, R./LeFurgy, J. *Boomburbs: The Rise of America's Accidental Cities*. Washington, DC: Brookings Institution Press. 2007.
7 Knox, P. *Metroburbia*. New Brunswick, NJ: Rutgers University Press. 2008.
8 Filion, P. "Suburban Morphology: Further Dispersion or Recentralization?" Manuscript. 2012. p. 2.
9 See for example, Alexander, C. *A Pattern Language: Towns, Buildings, Construction*. Oxford University Press, USA. 1977.
   Gutenberg, A. "A Multiple Land Use Classification System." In: *Journal of the American Institute of Planners*. 1959. 25(3).
10 Saunders, P. *Social Theory and the Urban Question*. Routledge. 1989.
    Castells, M. *The City and the Grassroots: A Cross-cultural Theory of Urban Social Movements*. Berkeley: University of California Press. 1983.
11 Storper, S./Walker, R. *The Capitalist Imperative: Territory, Technology, and Industrial Growth*. New York: Basil Blackwell. 1989.

12 Soja, E. "Inside Exopolis: Scenes from Orange County." In: Sorkin, M. *Variation on a Theme Park*. Noonday Press. 1992.
13 Zukin, S. *Landscapes of Power*. Berkeley and Los Angeles: UC Press. 1991.
14 Ibid., p. 17.
15 Dear, M. J. /Flusty, S. "Postmodern Urbanism." In: *Annals of the Association of American Geographers*. 2000. 90(1). p. 50–72.
16 Hitz, H./Keil, R./Lehrer, U./ Ronneberger, K./Schmid, C./ Wolff, R. *Capitale Fatales: Urbanisierung und Politik in den Finanzmetropolen Zürich und Frankfurt*. Zürich: Rotpunkt-Verlag. 1995.
17 Keil, R./Wood, P./ Young, D. (eds.): *In-Between Infrastructure: Urban Connectivity in an Age of Vulnerability*. Praxis (e)Press. 2011.
18 Young, D./Keil, R. "Reconnecting the In-between City." In: *New Geography*. 2010. http://www.newgeography.com/content/001497-reconnecting-in-between-city, 04.04.13.
19 Simone, A. *For the City Yet to Come: Changing African Life in Four Cities*. Durham and London: Duke Press. 2004.
20 Glaeser, E. *Triumph of the City: How our Greatest Invention Makes Us Richer, Smarter, Greener, Healthier, and Happier*. London: Penguin Press. 2011.
21 Larup, L. *One Million Acres & No Zoning*. London: AA Publications. 2011 .
22 de Jong, F. "The Bounded Megalopolis." In: *Centro vs Periphería*, Dossier 11.2012. p. 89–93.

SUBURBAN REDEVELOPMENT: DECLINE AND RENEWAL IN TORONTO'S IN-BETWEEN CITY

Douglas Young

Newly developed suburbs can appear attractive in a number of ways. They offer a pattern of buildings and land use quite different from that of central areas, a peripheral location considered "close to nature," an overall shiny newness of buildings, landscape and infrastructure, and for their first residents the sense of embarking on a new way of living. But over time, those suburbs lose their patina of newness and take up different positions in the mental maps of their respective urban regions. While some settle into a reputation of attractive maturity, others slip several rungs on the ladder of desirability becoming devalorized in comparison to other districts in their respective city-regions: the successive waves of newer suburbs and the gentrified and/or hip neighborhoods in the city's center.

Whether the modestly scaled point towers in the Stockholm satellite city Vällingby, the endless blocks of identical socialist-era pre-fab housing at the edge of every city in Eastern Europe, or Levittown, Long Island's tiny bungalows, the legacies of twentieth century sub-urbanisms confront us with the question of how to live with them today. That confronta-tion raises questions of the desirability or possibility of revitalization, renewal and redevel-opment. In the case of Toronto, for example, many districts that were developed as suburbs in the few decades following the end of the Second World War are now perceived to be in trouble; places of increasing poverty, inadequate public transit, and public and private hous-ing complexes in dire need of expensive retrofits. But at a time when their social need is so great and their physical disrepair is so extensive, a widespread and well-funded response to the problem of Toronto's postwar suburbs appears unlikely to materialize.

Toronto's troubled "inner suburbs" were intended by 1950s planning visionaries to be so-lutions to suburban problems of the day. They determined that the modern suburb of the 1960s should be more urban than earlier suburbs with higher densities, a physical mix of low- and high-rise buildings, and a social mix of private market and public housing. The end result was a vast in-between city[1] developed between the 1950s and 1980s. It was typi-cally suburban in some ways (with bungalows, shopping plazas and wide arterial roads) and typically urban in others (high-rise apartment buildings and a substantial amount of public housing). Today, those suburban districts appear as hybrids of city and suburb noteworthy for the hundreds of high-rise apartment buildings lining the main roads that act as bound-aries of inward-facing, low-rise neighborhoods.

Shoppers Drug Mart: the hybrid
landscape of the in-between
city, Toronto (2008)
Source: Roger Keil

Much has changed since then, including the people who live in those districts (now increasingly poor and racialized), ideas about what constitutes "good planning" and "good neighborhoods," and attitudes about the potential for, and desirability of, state-directed change. Empirical evidence of the deterioration of everyday life in Toronto's in-between city has been documented in several reports,[2] and in popular discourse, the "inner suburb" has become an urban problem just as the "inner city" was deemed to be fifty years ago. And just as programs of Urban Renewal were unleashed on the inner cities in many countries in the mid-twentieth century in response to a widely perceived need for action, the need for suburban renewal is felt in many cities today, including Toronto. But whether that need will be met is unclear.

A close look at the current debates about suburban decline and renewal in Toronto and other cities is revealing of evolving trends in urban governance (particularly related to urban planning), urban policy (particularly housing policy), and the place of suburbs in the overall urban region (place defined discursively and materially). Those trends make explicit the painful reality of the impact of decades of neoliberalism on suburban living. The retreat from principles of universality, active state interventionism, and social welfare in favor of individual self-regulation and the marketization of services has led directly to the impoverishment of everyday life in Toronto's in-between city.

At the same time, that general retreat makes an effective response to those resultant conditions challenging if not impossible. That this contradiction plays out so extensively in what were intended to have been model modern districts forces a general rethink of what life in them could be like. If they are no longer the suburbs they once were, what are they? What could they be? What precisely is the problem and what is the best solution to it?

While the general neoliberalization of urban governance restrains state intervention in response to the perception of suburban decline, it doesn't mean there is no governing by governments, or that, in the specific case of Toronto's postwar suburbs, the call for suburban revitalization goes unheeded. While it is true that governments do not govern all the time, "[o]n the other hand, there is rarely no government at all."[3] The challenge is to determine "*What* part, sector, group of the city is really governed? What is weakly governed? What is left out? What is escaping government?"[4]

While neoliberalism is often "(mis) represented as an authorless, omnipresent, and monolithic phenomenon,"[5] the processes of neoliberalization are, in fact, "open-ended" and "incomplete."[6] Following Theodore and Peck, we should seek:

> …to expose and problematize the actually existing character of different modalities and manifestations of neoliberalism, as a *constructed* project, and to denaturalize neoliberal urbanism as a policy paradigm by exploring its origins, its evolution, and its variegated form.[7]

Neoliberalism, they say, is "a mongrel mode of governance, always involving (flawed) state action and always interpenetrated with its others."[8] Typical of all modes of neoliberal governance is that the "urban paradox" — "the spatial coexistence of dynamic economic development and rising social inequalities" which Theodore and Peck consider "a quite predictable feature of neoliberal urbanism"[9] — is addressed at the local scale and with reliance on third sector and volunteer actors by "the adoption of bounded, local experimentation as a preferred mode of policy development."[10]

In the case of Toronto, a trio of policy initiatives launched by municipal government in recent years constitute a de facto and uncoordinated suburban renewal program. Tower Renewal, Transit City and Priority Neighborhoods taken together suggest that the "problem of the inner suburb" (or what Theodore and Peck might call the urban paradox of Toronto's suburbs) has risen to near the top of the local policy agenda. The promise of the Tower Renewal program is rehabilitation of all high-rise rental apartment buildings across the city regardless of location (going against the grain of property capital's cherry-picking of attractive sites at which to invest in building upgrades or site redevelopment). Transit City offers a vision of new light rail transit lines linking different parts of the in-between city to each other as well as to the historic downtown. Together, those two programs offer at least the hope of a greatly improved everyday life in Toronto's in-between city; material improvements to hundreds of thousands of dwellings, and improved connectedness to social and economic opportunity. Priority Neighborhoods is a program that targets thirteen of the city's socially most needy districts (out of a total of 140 neighborhoods), most of which are in the postwar suburban in-between city. While burdened with the contradictory implications of all place-based policy, Priority Neighborhoods nevertheless channels funding into several postwar suburban districts in Toronto.

But just as 1950s and 60s, urban renewal involved multiple actors with different motivations, and contradictory and highly contested methods and outcomes, de facto suburban renewal in Toronto, even as it is barely off the ground, can be similarly problematized. Each of the component parts of the concept — inner suburb, decline, renewal — can be questioned. Inner or older suburb suggests a place that is marked with failure in the sense of having lost the attraction of newness. Decline is as much a discursive as a material concept used, in part, to capture a cultural distaste for the hybrid spaces of the in-between city, particularly the forty- and fifty-year-old high-rise apartment slabs. To policymakers, renewal of declining older suburbs is best achieved through private sector redevelopment. The high-rise suburban rental buildings not lucky enough to be located on or near higher order transit lines or close to attractive natural features like Lake Ontario (and thus of little interest to property capital) become a kind of welfare caseload with which the city as social worker is saddled.

The City of Toronto's Tower Renewal (TR) program originated in building science classes held at the University of Toronto in 2000, which studied the need to re-skin the city's aging high-rise apartment buildings[11] and was eventually taken up and championed by David Miller, Toronto's mayor from 2003 to 2007. Approximately 1,100 high-rise residential rental buildings constructed in the city between the 1950s and early 1980s contain more than 300,000 units and are home to at least 500,000 people. Tower Renewal makes the case that, as a vast stock of relatively affordable housing, they constitute an invaluable social resource warranting attention and investment. Proponents of TR point to examples of successful building renewal and community development programs in high-rise suburban districts in many European cities as policy models for Toronto to emulate. While TR appears intuitively to be a good idea, there are many different perspectives on high-rise residential buildings in Toronto and what renewing them means.

To the building scientist, renewal is a question of a total retrofit of building skin and building systems to make greener buildings. While the towers' concrete structures have a life expectancy of 300 to 400 years,[12] their skins and building systems need retrofitting every fifty or sixty years and it is now time for the first retrofit. From this perspective, the success of Tower Renewal would be measured against quantifiable building performance standards. To private sector building owners, renewal in the form of capital upgrades is necessary in order to protect the asset from falling apart and to protect its reputation. To an owner, successful TR would require a minimal capital investment while allowing the building to continue

High-rise neighborhood,
Thorncliffe Park, Toronto (2012)
Source: Roger Keil

to be leveraged to purchase other buildings. To the social advocacy agency, United Way, suburban tower neighborhoods are geographic concentrations of poverty that require place-based policy. To the local housing authority, Toronto Community Housing, the suburban towers in their portfolio represent a maintenance backlog headache totaling several hundred million dollars. To planners and architects, TR provides the opportunity to reimagine neighborhoods as "complete communities" with new facilities, services and dwelling types not included in their initial development several decades ago. To tower residents, successful TR would take the form of the material upgrading of the locus of everyday life: replacing broken down elevators and leaky windows, renovating their kitchens and bathrooms, re-pairing cracks and leaks and eliminating mold. Tower Renewal as a concept is pushed and pulled in many directions. Can the different directions intersect, or will only the easiest paths be followed?

As admirable as the many goals of Tower Renewal are, it presents some striking contradictions revealing of its particular form of "mongrel governance." First, it attempts to achieve public social policy (improvements to the quality of housing stock) through the private market. Second, and linked to the first, it is an attempt at launching a new government initiative that involves the private market in an era (neoliberal) and an arena (privately owned rental housing) that resist government initiative. Specifically, it proposes an alignment ("mongrel," in the words of Theodore and Peck) of state, market and civil society that would see the state use its ability to raise capital in order to provide low-interest loans to private landlords to upgrade their buildings with the aim of preserving a large stock of relatively affordable housing.

It paints a win-win scenario in which landlords end up with enhanced assets, tenants end up with improved buildings while avoiding dramatic rent increases, and the city successfully deals with a city-wide concern at no net cost to taxpayers. But in elevating preservation of the existing private sector rental housing stock to be seen as the key to addressing the housing affordability crisis, it indirectly undermines the possibility of building support for the creation of a well-funded program of new social housing construction in Ontario (a province in which programs for building new social housing were halted in 1995). As well, TR may in fact lead to diminished affordability if significant building upgrades ultimately translate into rent increases.

The role government has carved out for itself in the debates over decline and renewal in Toronto's in-between city is a decidedly self-limiting one. It tries to create conditions that will attract private sector interest in renewal while shunning a direct role for itself in under-taking widespread suburban renewal. For example, the city is loosening the regulatory planning framework that governs the high-rise districts in the in-between city in the hope that property capital will respond with proposals for infill development. Planners argue that the "'legacy' zoning by-laws of the 1960s and 1970s that still govern land use in Toronto's apartment neighborhoods severely limit potential changes and are hampering reinvestment."[13]

Rigid zoning, it is claimed, is one reason those neighborhoods "lack many of the hallmarks of 'complete communities' ... including access to fresh food; opportunities for entrepreneurs and social enterprise: employment; and many of the facilities and services fundamental to families, such as child care."[14]

At the same time, the advocates of zoning changes just as clearly note that "barriers to investment in apartment neighborhoods are not solely limited to, nor the principal responsibility of, the existing zoning framework. A multitude of socioeconomic, demographic, real estate capital market, site constraints, and other forces, shape and influence the viability of investment in all communities."[15] In other words, the proposed zoning changes are acknowledged by their proponents to be but one tiny potential trigger of renewal, but in light of the general limitation of direct state action they are nevertheless considered worth pursuing.

Interestingly, the "best practices" cited as role models for Toronto's suburban renewal — for example the *Stadtumbau* program in Germany — was possible only because of very generous funding from senior governments (state and federal). While Toronto's TR proponents laud the results of that and similar programs undertaken in European cities, they appear to have overlooked the significant difference when compared to the Toronto program in terms of the role of government as actor in the process. The unfortunate reality of Suburban

East Scarborough Storefront   Source: Roger Keil
Community Centre,
Scarborough District,
Toronto (2010)

Renewal in Toronto's in-between city is that the particular mongrel mode of governance that has evolved will necessarily be insufficient to address social and physical need in anything but a piecemeal and fragmented manner.

Endnotes

1 Sieverts, T. *Cities Without Cities: an Investigation of the Zwischenstadt.* Ondon: Spon.2003.

2 United Way Toronto. *Poverty by Postal Code 2: Vertical Poverty. Declining Income, Housing Quality and Community Life in Toronto's Inner Suburban High-Rise Apartments.* Toronto: United Way. 2011. United Way Toronto. *Poverty by Postal Code.* Toronto: United Way. 2004.

3 Borraz, O./LeGalès, P. "Urban Governance in Europe: The Government of What?" In: Pôle Sud. 32(1). 2010. p.138–139.

4 Ibid., p. 139. Emphasis added.

5 Theodore, N./ Peck, J. "Framing Neoliberal Urbanism: Translating 'Commonsense' Urban Policy Across the OECD Zone." In: *European Urban and Regional Studies.* 19 (1). 2011. p. 21.

6 Ibid.

7 Ibid., Emphasis in original.

8 Ibid., p. 24.

9 Ibid., p. 38.

10 Ibid., p. 38.

11 Kesik, Ted (2011) Personal interview. Feb. 14, 2011, Toronto.

12 Ibid.

13 (CUG) Centre for Urban Growth and Community. *Strong Neighbourhoods and Complete Communities: a New Approach to Zoning for Apartment Neighbourhoods.* Toronto. 2012. p. 2.

14 Ibid.

15 Ibid.

SUBURBAN BOUNDARIES: BEYOND GREENBELTS AND EDGES

Roger Keil & Rob Shields

Thinking about suburbanization and suburbanisms can be an exercise in addressing "boundaries." The transition from city to countryside has always been a critical interface of human existence. Since antiquity, the inside/outside problematic has been a central spatial concern of urbanism: walls, moats, gates. Boundaries have forever defined the urban.

The German word *Stadtkante* (city edge) denotes the stark spatiality of separation that defined urban reality over the course of European history. The *Stadtkante* lives on in the imaginaries on the European city beyond Weber's town, Simmel's metropolis, and even Howard's Garden City. In North America, by contrast, the concentric circles of the Chicago school peter out in the non-descript sprawling periurbanity that defined the Fordist "suburban solution" of the twentieth century.[1]

The Los Angeles School has proposed to replace this hierarchical circularity by a more fractal and fragmented model.[2] Yet even here, the desert frontier will be reached sooner rather than later. Historically, as Jon Teaford reminds us, "suburbs have existed virtually as long as cities," and have been the space of both desire and fear, freedom and displacement: "The fringe represented freedom from the city — the ability to do what was not allowed or impossible within the densely-populated core."[3] The fringe, moreover, has two faces, one directed back towards the city, one looking outward towards the world beyond. It is this space that suburbs have traditionally occupied as zones of transition, where meaning was negotiated through codes that were urban-emergent, not yet entirely urban, but clearly not rural anymore.

Ironically, suburbs as urban edges are dependent on specific understandings of boundaries. We have to draw a boundary around suburbs to define our area of study. But there are two distinct understandings of boundary. The first, casts it as a limit between an inside and outside, as in the example of *Stadtkante*. As an interface, it is not only an edge but has the qualities of a surface. This membrane or interface both divides and is a screen on which an interior is projected, visible to the exterior and vice versa. It thus mediates and structures what passes between these two areas or states, the urban and rural.

In this view, the very possibility of defining and thereby reflecting on our experience of sub-urbanism and the phenomena of periurban environments is dependent on the construction of suburbia as a category and its contrast with other environmental and spatial categories. Heidegger and others argue that boundary drawing is constitutive in categorization. "A boundary is not that at which something stops but … the boundary is that from which something begins its presencing."[4]

Boundaries, then, are historico-spatial products of relationships between urban activities and non-urban activities. Needless to say, this kind of dichotomous thinking needs to be in-terrogated in a postsuburban world.[5] In urban society, the rural and the urban are sublated into a new quality of which city, boundary and fringe are mere elements of a reassembled synthetic future which persists as a moment of "disorientation."[6] Boundaries are acts of dif-ferentiation and identification[7] that allow us to establish the terms of relationships between identities.[8] These edges are understood as Euclidean geometric surfaces and it is from its edge that we first know the city.

A second approach casts the boundary as a limit in the sense of a bifurcation or sudden change of state, such as the line of a fold across a surface. The fold is the most basic of top-ological transformations. It creates a threshold or transition between the two areas. Like a folded piece of paper, as entities cross the vertice — the *Kante* ("ledge") — they are precipi-tously reoriented in a different geometry of relationships even though they continue on and in the exact same surface and set of flows. These edges are topological in the sense that they deal not with breaks or divisions but with transformations that occur without fundamental ruptures or divisions between, for example, "inside" and "outside." That is, this conception of boundary emphasizes transition and the junctural.

Examples of these different boundary topologies in suburbia can be found in the cases of geographical barriers such as freeways, rivers, farmland, and greenbelts. These may define suburbs, however perceived divisions such as major roads equally allow any neighborhood to function as an enclave. For suburban youth, for example, residence in a given neighbor-hood is an easy basis for both social affiliation and identity. Futrell and Simi refer to these as "prefigurative spaces" of "small, locally-bound, interpersonal networks where members engage in political socialization, boundary marking, and other cultural practices."[9] That is, material and perceived boundaries in the landscape support local "boundary marking, and other cultural practices [that] allow members to participate in relationships that 'prefigure' their desired vision for social life and the city on a broader scale."[10] These boundaries are as much identifications around a specific area as they are boundaries against dominant culture or subordinate groups. The extreme example would be the geographies of exclusion created by gated communities and "*condominos*."[11]

Suburbia as a boundary-space plays host to a plethora of "boundary-objects," defined as entities inhabiting intersecting worlds and satisfying the informational requirements of each of them. "Boundary objects are … both plastic enough to adapt to local needs and the constraints of the several parties employing them, yet robust enough to maintain a common identity."[12]

Although they consider boundary objects to be mobile in Euclidean, three-dimensional space, it is equally possible to understand boundary objects as static in the everyday sense of the term but yet resident in intersecting spaces with quite different dimensionalities such as might be found in the situation of a threshold. Boundary objects are thus always ambiguous when defined within a static point of view such as an urban growth model.

Greenbelts, official reserves of agricultural, park, and natural land, illustrate the ambiguity of boundary objects: mapped on a two-dimensional chart, they can take the form of a belt-like edge, limiting the city. However, experienced in three-dimensions, these marooned ecosystems are often spatial fragments of rural landscape anchored within the urban order of zoning and city growth over time. Walter Prigge's study of the Frankfurt Greenbelt, following Benjamin, as a "transition" or "threshold" is to be differentiated sharply from the conventional idea of boundary.[13] The threshold has a spatial quality; it is not just a line. Related concepts are zone, change, transition. The idea of a liminal zone is not far from this concept.[14] They seem to be spaces where "the ambiguous" (*Zweideutiges*) replaces "the actual" (*das Eigentliche*).[15] Prigge notes that "on the threshold two different spaces overlap: it is open to both, free from the unilateral constraints of the one or the other, however touched by the determinations and uses of both."[16] Crossing the threshold changes the perspective (there are reverberations here of Benjamin's famous dreamspaces). The interdependency between actual material and ideal cultural boundaries links barriers in the material landscape and divisions between categories. Lefebvre grants the material preeminence in a trialectic between material practices of space and phenomena, narrative discourses on space and the framing quality of imagined spaces of possibility.[17] However, insofar as a neighborhood is an imagined space, it also has identification and performative qualities. In practice, this can yield a boundary breakdown between the ideal and actual or the discursive and material that makes the suburb much less easy to define by drawing boundaries in one register or in one classificatory schema.

The greenbelt-as-threshold points to the central contradictions of modern metropolitanity of which suburbanization is a major factor. We now encounter "fragmented places and histories" and "'city', 'land', 'center' and 'periphery' [become] obsolete concepts."[18] Perhaps this is a good threshold from which to understand the relationship of greenbelts and suburbs more generally? Suburbanization is now so pervasive that it is present on both sides of the greenbelt, which poses questions of inside/outside relations. In fact, this reminds one of Reyner Banham's[19] famous observation that when drivers enter Los Angeles by exiting the freeway and switching to surface roads, they cross the boundary between the outside and the inside. Rather than a hard line, this is now a space for multifaceted negotiation. Similarly, the greenbelt becomes an instance of the kind of "rural urbanism," which Laura Barraclough has examined in the San Fernando Valley in Los Angeles, in which "rurality, suburbia, and urbanity have coexisted, often tensely… [in a] distinctive mélange of rural, suburban, and urban landscapes."[20]

The dynamics of the boundary setting that greenbelts perform in an era of global suburbanization are vastly different in various places. In the old brownfield industrial landscapes of Birmingham and the Emscher, grass grows literally over the ruins of an obsolete spatial fix. In the booming regions of Toronto, Frankfurt, Seoul, and Gurgaon, greenbelts are expansion spaces and projection screens for the global city.[21] In the case of the Canadian oil town of Fort McMurray, Alberta, we find a particular "feral suburbanism" without much of a boundary between the vinyl suburban world of universal subdivisions and the bogs and swamps of an unforgiving nature just beyond.[22]

Another central terrain for negotiation of city and non-city is the political and social ecology of the greenbelt. While we can imagine the metabolism of the urban region as a seamless web of human and non-human life with metabolic streams connecting organisms, we also must recognize the obstacles and facilitating channels by which those streams are conditioned and sustainabilities are fixed.[23] The greenbelt, as a negotiated space of societal relationships of nature that connect urban and non-urban activities, becomes an additional

Eagle Ridge is a recent suburban development in Fort McMurray that has both low-rise condominiums and single-family homes. The latter may be occupied by single families, but often households take in boarder(s) to help pay the mortgage (2010).

Source: Claire Major

canvas for the production of (social/urban) nature where suburbanization and urbanization are enclosed, enabled and energized.

Lefebvre notes that "urban society can only be defined as global" and maintains further that "it covers the planet by recreating nature."[24] Under these conditions, the urbanized region develops in a rather patchwork, in-between way.[25] Yet, as John Friedmann points out, a greenbelt contains an ethics of enclosure; the metaphor of the belt is one of control over flows.[26] How realistic and how sustainable is that in today's world? Can this really be a boundary that holds? This relates ultimately to the relationship of agriculture and the city: the infrastructure of the agricultural mode of production now becomes a new spatial fix for the post(sub)urban realities of the regional metropolis. The greenbelt holds as a boundary for suburban development and becomes the dreamspace threshold for alternative uses of green space. Instead of agriculture, we are now getting para-agriculture. Horse farms, trailer parks, Christmas tree plantations, apple-picking farms, and fall festivals replace the traditional agricultural activities that structured the landscape of the greenbelt over many generations.

The landscape beyond the city in which greenbelts have been established has long been rural. The infrastructures laid out there have facilitated agricultural production and, in the cases of Birmingham and the Emscher, also industrial or mining activities. In this sense, the greenbelts' matrix has been inscribed in physical and social terms as non-urban. Yet

Welcome to Uxbridge:
A Greenbelt Community (2012)
Source: Roger Keil

today's greenbelts have to be seen not as qualitatively different from urban structures and relationships but rather as conjugations of the urban and rural and other postsuburban relationships. The design and use of those greenbelts today are taking shape not *against* but *in conversation with* the push of the surrounding suburbs. The use of infrastructure in the greenbelt is no longer governed by the primacy of agricultural pursuits, but by the interests of urbanites in real and imagined green landscapes.

Where does this take us? Suburbanization redefines urban boundaries conceptually and physically. Chief among those is the constantly changing relationship of nature and urban society. Metropolitan governance works those boundaries through buffer zones (greenbelts, wedges, fingers,[27] urban national parks) that contain and govern suburban expansion and/or conserve natural or agricultural landscapes around metropolitan centers. Greenbelt initiatives are now imposing themselves on the political discourses of a variety of urban areas around the world. In Toronto, Birmingham, the Ruhr, Frankfurt, Seoul, and Delhi/Gurgaon, such attempts at threshold politics are particularly visible.

Sieverts[28] sees the postindustrial as a space of new possibilities: at the scale of an entire landscape, greenbelts act as a focus for meaning making. They are the historical thresholds between industrial and postindustrial landscapes (e.g., Birmingham, Emscher).

Besides this temporal boundary between the modernism and industrialism of the previous period and the fragmented post-industrialism of the current period there are also now the spatial boundaries between different imaginaries in which the urban is refracted: is a golf course in the greenbelt urban, suburban, or rural?

Welcome to the Greenbelt: Source: Roger Keil
New residential development
at Ontario Greenbelt boundary
(2009)

At the heart of North American suburbia is exactly this hybridity of the city and the country. In addition, the degree to which areas are urbanized changes over time: parts of central Detroit are now classified as "rural" according to the US Census, due to the low density of residents. As suburbia changes over time, the nature and form of boundaries and their material markers changes from line to threshold in ways that can add to the ambiguity.

Spatially and temporally, suburbia can become "monstrous" (formless, *monstrere*): a cyborg.[29] This may be a case of the different boundaries or topological edges of a phenomenon not matching up. Thus it is possible to "play" across these understandings of the suburb as the limit of the city and as a notable edge within an environment that stretches from an urban to a rural condition. The notable feature of the figure of the cyborg is its ability to maintain an identity homeostatically across conditions and to thus integrate hybrids into a whole.

This makes suburbia an ideal space for artistic experimentation with the blurring of boundaries and the confusion of categories.[30] During the late twentieth century, suburban multiplex cinemas and IMAX theatres proliferated, offering in their scale, 3D and immersive qualities an aestheticized version of this lived experience[31] where the boundaries of the individual are merged into those of the experiential cinematic space in a kind of psychanaesthesia. Planners have been slower to recognize this experimental aspect of "creative suburbia."[32] Suburbia has generally been addressed according to its lack of urban density, features, and amenities, and its subordinate and dependent status in relation to an urban core, which is not the case in many cities where the suburban edge is the economic heart of an urban agglomeration.

Industry and energy meet:
Frankfurt GreenBelt south of the
Main River (2011)
Source: Roger Keil

Suburbia thus challenges us to rethink boundaries not as mere limits but as thresholds, fluid zones, and even as creative heartlands. This requires a topological imagination that grasps the boundary as a function within a larger spatial and temporal system or "cultural topology," rather than as the *Stadtkante* as a wall-like beginning or end of urban phenomena. This shift in understanding allows one to theorize the ambiguous status of the boundary as *Doppelkante*, "a doubled edge" if you will. It allows us to see that the boundary is as much a question of a reorientation of objects, folding them and the entire space from one dimension into another. This allows one to conceive of changes to the meaning of the same entity placed in the city-center, on its suburban margin, and in a rural area. It also allows us to begin to theorize the suburb as a research object, in that it is both a boundary object and a boundary-space itself.

Endnotes

1 Walker, R. *The Suburban Solution: Capitalism and the Construction of Urban Space in the United. States.* (unpublished Ph.D. thesis, Johns Hopkins University). 1977.
2 Judd, D.R. /Simpson, D. (eds.): The City Revisited: Urban Theory from Chicago, Los Angeles, New York. Minneapolis: University of Minnesota Press. 2011.
3 Teaford, J. C. "Suburbia and Post-suburbia: A Brief History." In: Phelps, N.A./ Wu, F. (eds.): *International Perspectives on Suburbanization: A Post-Suburban World?* London: Palgrave Macmillan. 2011. p. 15.
4 Heidegger, M. *Poetry Language Thought.* London: Harper and Row. 1975. p. 155.
5 Phelps, N.A./ Wu, F. (eds.) 2011. *International Perspectives on Suburbanization: A Post-Suburban World?* London: Palgrave Macmillan. 2011.
6 Lefebvre, H. *The Production of Space* (N. Donaldson-Smith, Trans.). Oxford: Basil Blackwell. 1991. p. 183.
7 Latour, B. *The Pasteurization of France Followed by Irreducations.* Cambridge: Harvard University Press. 1988. p.169.
8 Derrida, J." Point de Folie--Maintenant l'architecture." In: *La Casa Vide.* 1986; Law, J. *Organizing Modernity.* Oxford: Blackwell. 1994; Shields, R. *Places on the Margin: Alternative Geographies of Modernity.* London: Routledge Chapman Hall. 1991.
9 Futrell, R./Simi, P. "Free Spaces, Collective Identity, and the Persistence of US White Power Activism." In: *Social Problems 51,* 2004. p. 17.
10 Ibid. p. 16, cited in: Culton, K. R./Holtzman, B. "The Growth and Disruption of a 'Free Space': Examining a Suburban Do It Yourself (DIY) Punk Scene." In: *Space and Culture 13.* 2010. (3). p. 275.
11 Sibley, D. *Geographies of Exclusion.* London: Routledge. 1995.
12 Star, S. L./Greisemer, J. R. "Institutional Ecology, 'Translations' and Boundary Objects: Amateurs and Professionals in Berkeley's Museum of Vertebrate Zoology 1907-1939." In: *Social Studies of Science 19–* 1989.(4). p. 393.
13 Prigge, W. "Übergänge: Auf der Schwelle einer neuen Stadtentwicklungspolitik." In: Koenigs, T. (ed.): *Vision offener Grünräume: Grün-Gürtel Frankfurt.* Frankfurt & New York: Campus Verlag. 1991. p. 173–8; Also see: Menninghaus, W. *Schwellenkunde: Walter Benjamins Passage des Mythos.* Frankfurt. 1986.
14 Culton, K.R./Holtzman, B., 2010. Op. cit.
15 Prigge, 1991. Op.cit,. p. 173.
16 Prigge, 1991. Op. cit. p. 173.
17 Heidegger, M., 1975. Op. cit. p. 357.
18 Prigge, 1991. Op. cit. p. 175.
19 Banham, R. *Los Angeles: The Architecture of Four Ecologies.* 1970.
20 Barraclough, L.R. *Making the San Fernando Valley: Rural Landscapes, Urban Development, and White Privilege.* Athens & London: University of Georgia Press). 2011. p. 3.
21 Keil R./Ronneberger K. "Going up the Country: Internationalization and Urbanization on Frankfurt's Northern Fringe." In: *Environment and Planning D: Society and Space.* 1994. 12(2). p. 137–166.
22 Shields, R. "Feral Suburbs: Cultural Topologies of Social Reproduction, Fort McMurray, Canada." In: *International Journal of Cultural Studies.* 2012. 15 (3). p. 205–215.
23 Macdonald, S./ Keil, R. "The Ontario Greenbelt: Shifting the Scales of the Sustainability Fix?" In: *The Professional Geographer.2012. 64(2).* p. 1–21; Keil, R./ Whitehead, M. "Cities and the Politics of Sustainability." In: *Oxford Handbook of Urban Politics.* Oxford: OUP. 2012.
24 Heidegger, M., 1975. Op. cit. p. 167.
25 Sieverts, T. *Cities without Cities: An Interpretation of the Zwischenstadt.* London & New York: Routledge. 2003; Sieverts, T. "The In-Between City as an Image of Society: From the Impossible Order Towards a Possible Disorder in the Urban Landscape." In: Young, D./ Burke Wood , P./Keil, R. (eds.): *In-Between Infrastructure: Urban Connectivity in an Age of Vulnerability.* Kelowna. Praxis (e) Press. 2011; Sieverts, T. "On the Relations of Culture and Suburbia: How to Give Meaning to the Suburban Landscape?" In: Hamel, P./ Keil, R. (eds.): *Suburban Governance: A Global View.* Toronto: UTP. Forthcoming.
26 Friedmann, J. "Wem gehört er?" In: *Kommune.* 1991. 9(6). p. 36.
27 Ring, H. "A Guerrilla Greenbelt for London." In: Naik, D./Oldfield, T. (eds.): *Critical Cities 1* London:This is not a Gateway /Myrdle Court Press. 2009.
28 Ibid.
29 Haraway, D. "A Manifesto for Cyborgs: Science, Technology and Socialist Feminism in the 1980s." In: Nicholson, L.J. (ed.): *Feminism/Postmodernism.* 1990. p. 65–107.
30 Park, O. "Ambivalence and Strangeness in the Everyday Utopianism of Suburbia." In: *Public Journal, 43.* 2011.
31 Recuber, T. "Immersion Cinema: The Rationalization and Reenchantment of Cinematic Space." In: *Space and Culture 10.* 2007.(3). p. 315–330.
32 Flew, T. (2012). Creative Suburbia : Rethinking Urban Cultural Policy – The Australian Case. In: *International Journal of Cultural Studies 15.* 2010.(3). p. 231–246.

AUTOMOBILES, HIGHWAYS, AND SUBURBAN DISPERSION

Pierre Filion

Suburban parking lot:
York University, Toronto (2013)
Source: Roger Keil

Infrastructures have shaped the North American suburban form. The circumstances that have abetted the fullest emanation of a car-centered urban environment marked a radical break in the history of urban form. The dispersion (absence of multifunctional centers and a scattering of activities in a functionally specialized and primarily low-density environment) of the post Second World War suburb contrasts with prior centralized patterns.[1] As most postwar development conformed to this model, newer metropolitan regions are primarily dispersed in nature. Hence the replacement of the centralized Chicago model by the dispersed Los Angeles model as the current representation of North American urbanization.[2]

The car-dependent North American suburban form was pieced together in the fifteen years or so following the Second World War.[3] In a climate of robust economic growth, accelerated demographic expansion, pent-up demand for consumer goods and forceful lobbying from the car and oil industry, the different aspects of the suburb were devised over this period. It may be difficult to acknowledge, at a time when the postwar suburban model comes under harsh criticism, that it was inspired by utopian visions. Foreseeing the dramatic rise in urban accessibility a generalized use of the automobile would afford, a succession of urban visions relying on innovative car-oriented transportation systems and offering plentiful space and greenery were formulated over the 1930s. The most eminent were Frank Lloyd Wright's Broadacre City and Futurama, a diorama prepared by Norman Bel Geddes for the 1939–1940 New York World's Fair.[4] None of these utopian visions anticipated the full implication of total dependence on the automobile, however. Utopias from the 1930s failed to preview congestion and the large amounts of space taken over by parking. Little wonder that suburban development did not unfold in accordance with these visions.

A number of causal mechanisms connect the rapidly rising automobile dependency of the postwar period with the dispersed morphology of the suburb. Efforts at accommodating the car shifted previous accessibility patterns, associated with a predominance of public transit. The tendency for public transit networks to adopt radial configurations and the capacity of these services to funnel large numbers of people to a single destination fostered centralization. In North America the public transit metropolis featured a strong central business district (CBD), where office employment, institutions, mass and high-order retailing, culture, and entertainment clustered. In contrast, generalized automobile use breeds decentralization and causes a flattening of accessibility gradients, notwithstanding minor peaks at expressway exits. Such accessibility patterns discourage the creation of centers and therefore lend themselves to a dispersion of activities. They also free residential areas from the need to trade off space consumption in order to maintain strong ties with the CBD, and they thus make it possible for households to consume much more land.

The large amounts of space required to accommodate a generalized use of the car also shape suburban form. Not only were certain types of buildings modified to suit the car (e.g., drive-through establishments), but all structures had to comply with formulas assuring sufficient parking space.[5] The most obvious impact on suburban morphology was a decline in density caused by the need to provide space for cars. Retailing and offices, two land uses formerly known for their compactness, were particularly affected by this phenomenon. The presence of large amounts of cars separates activities, inhibiting potential synergy effects. Frequent interactions between close-by activities typical of traditional downtowns rely on pedestrian movements and thereby on a walking-conducive environment.[6] Large parking expanses surrounding suburban activities rule out such interactions and thereby the very existence of well-functioning, multiuse centers. Herein lies another factor accounting for the dispersion of activities in North American suburbs.

Not only is the automobile orientation of suburbs adverse to multiuse centers due to flattened accessibility patterns and the space taken by cars, but it is also contrary to the very concept of multifunctionality. Negative externalities generated by traffic flows are sources of conflicts between activities that used to blend with each other. Land uses that are not otherwise sources of nuisance — such as retailing, offices and even places of worship — need to be isolated from residential areas because of the large amount of cars they attract.

At the heart of the postwar suburban formula is the super-grid configuration, whose purpose is to channel traffic on arterials and provide tranquil residential havens within resulting super-blocks. Conceptually, the super-grid formula consists of arterials laid out between one and two kilometers from each other. In reality, while the essence of the formula is generally respected, geographical and jurisdictional obstacles, as well as planning inventiveness, often preclude the emergence of symmetrical super-grids. Inside super-blocks, road patterns often adopt a curvilinear layout in order to discourage through traffic. The

The urbanization of the
Don Valley giving flight to the
suburbs (2012)
Source: Stephen Mak

super-grid configuration encourages the specialization of suburban land uses thanks to the role arterials play in preventing the spill-over of negative externalities. It follows that super blocks are typically devoted to a single land use or few compatible types of activities and that the partitioning role of arterials makes it possible to locate incompatible activities in abutting super-blocks.[7]

While those aspects of the suburb that promote mutual adaptation between automobile-oriented transportation and dispersed land use were all in place early on in the evolution of the postwar suburb, this adaptive relationship has become further entrenched over time. Creativity in tailoring land uses to an automobile-dominated environment drove this evolution. Among recent illustrations of this process are big box stores, power malls, mega supermarkets and multiplex cinemas, all of which rely on a large catchment area of drivers.

It would be a mistake to overlook the positive aspects of the North American suburban model, for without understanding them it is impossible to comprehend why this formula has spread so rapidly and thoroughly across the continent. First, the suburban model has proven to be exceptionally efficient at supplying developable land, thus assuring the affordability of home ownership for the middle class and providing reasonably priced premises for businesses. One only need observe the wide diversity of establishments along the homely suburban retail strip to realize the contribution the marriage between automobile accessibility and cheap land makes to economic development. Second, as activities decentralized to the suburb and everywhere downtowns lost ground in relative (and in many cases in absolute) terms, suburbs became the prime location to access work, retailing and services. Third, the suburban formula has proven successful at providing residential areas that are highly valued by their occupants, as revealed by surveys on residential satisfaction.[8] And finally, the standardized nature of suburbs, where development takes place by replication (whereby new areas reproduce the morphology and distribution of activities found in previously developed sectors), eases suburban growth.

A number of circumstances have caused the suburban model to lose its varnish, prompting a chorus of complaints about suburban form and lifestyle. In many places, the accessible suburb utopia has given way to the congested suburb reality. Expressways and arterials are saturated by the rising number and length of car journeys, largely a function of the distribution of suburban activities. The deteriorating economy of recent decades, resulting in a compression of the middle class and tighter public sector budgets, makes it difficult for many households to face the expense of total car dependency and for public administrations to maintain and expand suburban highway networks.

Criticism of suburbs also stems from awareness of the adverse health effects of the sedentary suburban lifestyle. Long distances between activities and the general unsuitability of suburban environments for other modes rule out most alternatives to the car. There is also mounting awareness of environmental damages inflicted by suburban areas, especially the emission of greenhouse gases by road transportation.

Finally, the vulnerability inherent in the suburban model is a growing source of concern. Not only are its infrastructures expensive to develop and maintain, but its transportation system is at the mercy of the numerous circumstances that can disrupt oil supply and cause skyrocketing energy prices. There may be reasons to link the frequently observed political conservatism of suburban dwellers to feelings of insecurity.[9]

Given the problems associated with the car-dependent and dispersed nature of suburbs, it is not surprising that planners advance as a solution a recentralization strategy accompanied with public transit expansion. Virtually all metropolitan-scale plans from North American urban regions with a population over one million propose some form of recentralization. It involves the further development or creation of multifunctional centers that are walking friendly and connected to new or improved public transit systems. These centers are proposed at different scales: from metropolitan-wide downtowns and nodal networks to neighborhood community centers. Plans underscore a number of advantages associated with the recentralization strategy: reduced land consumption and environmental impacts; increased diversity in transportation options, land use patterns and therefore lifestyles; the economic development potential of synergy and multi-functionality.[10]

There are reasons for the stark discrepancy between the importance given to recentralization in plans and the enduring dispersed nature of suburban development. Above all, it is difficult to break from the prevailing suburban land use transportation dynamics. For example, the introduction of quality public transit in a dispersed environment, where origins and destinations are scattered, is costly and unlikely to make a dent in modal shares. Likewise, efforts to foster pedestrian- and transit-conducive development in new centers run a high risk of being dashed by the low-density and dispersed nature of the catchment areas of these centers, which means that the car will occupy much of their space. Recentralization strategies would also need to confront the massive sums sunk in the suburban form over the past seventy years. The present slow economic growth and resulting tight public sector budgets would thus make it difficult to reverse or just alter prevailing patterns of development. This observation is especially relevant to the high cost of establishing public transit systems, of sufficient quality to compete with the car, in order to modify modal shares and encourage suburban developments that are multifunctional and with densities exceeding substantially present suburban norms.

At the time when US economic influence was at its peak, American consultants were spreading the automobile-focused urban transportation gospel across the world. But we have observed the rising critiques directed at the automobile-dominated suburban form and the difficulties in retrofitting this model, which begs the question: where will solutions to suburban transportation come from?

Even in North America, a number of metropolitan regions adopted a balanced transportation strategy, supporting both highways and quality public transit (subways, commuter trains, and LRTs). In most instances, public transit investment followed the completion of expressway networks. But the fullest manifestations of a balanced strategy are found in Europe, where vast transit projects have maintained high public transit modal shares in a context of elevated incomes and car ownership.[11] The success of this strategy was aided by stable funding streams and higher metropolitan (including suburban) densities than in North America. Presently, developing Asian nations share this approach.

Another transportation option consists in substantial low-cost public transit improvements. The creation of extensive BRT networks in Curitiba and Bogota are the foremost examples of this type of approach, which is gaining ground in the global south.[12] Finally, with the creation of dedicated lanes, the popularity of cycling has risen in many cities. Still, in most cases cycling modal shares remain marginal, although cycling use equals or exceeds that of other modes in some exceptional instances. After walking, cycling is the most cost-effective form of transportation from both a public and personal finance perspective. It works best where adapted infrastructures are present and in compact urban areas where distances are relatively short, such as Amsterdam and Copenhagen, the finest examples of cycling-oriented cities.[13]

While the contemporary suburb often owes its existence to highways connecting urban areas to national and international networks, the availability of public transit therein typically lags behind development. It follows that because of their distance from centralized metropolitan activities (main transit destinations) and their location at or beyond the extremity of public transit lines, suburbs suffer from a transit accessibility deficit relative to older parts, whatever the quality of systems in place at a metropolitan scale.

Yet, it is obvious that suburbs that are relatively dense, present some centralization and are serviced by quality public transit, offer more life style options, are better adapted to the present polarization of incomes and problematic public finances, and offer more resilience in the face of possible energy crises than the low-density automobile-oriented suburban model.

Endnotes

1   Filion, P./Bunting, T./Warriner, K.."The Entrenchment of Urban Dispersion: Residential Location Patterns and Preferences in the Dispersed City." *Urban Studies.* (36). 1996. p. 1317–1347.
2   Dear, M.J./Flusty, S. "Los Angeles as Postmodern Urbanism,: In: Dear, M. J. (ed.): *From Chicago to L.A.: Making Sense of Urban Theory.* Thousand Oaks: Sage. 2001. p. 55–83.
3   Rowe, P. G. *Making a Middle Landscape.* Cambridge: MIT Press. 1991.
4   Rydell, R. W./ Burd Schiavo, L. (eds.): *Designing Tomorrow: America's World's Fairs of the 1930s.* New Haven: Yale University Press. 2010
5   Shoup, D.C. *The High Cost of Free Parking.* Chicago: Planners Press, American Planning Association. 2005
6   Thomson, J. M. *Great Cities and Their Traffic.* London: Gollancz. 1977
7   Filion, P. "Evolving Suburban Morphology: Dispersion or Recentralization?" In: *Urban Morphology.*16. 2012. p. 101–119.
8   Clark, W./Deurloo, M./Dieleman, F. "Residential Mobility and Neighbourhood Outcomes." In: *Housing Studies.* 21. 2006. p. 323–342.
9   Walks, A. "The Causes of City-Suburban Political Polarization? A Canadian Case Study." In: *Annals of the Association of American Geographers.* 96. 206. p. 390–414.
10 Filion, P./Kramer, A. "Urban Intensification Models and Metropolitan-Scale Planning in the US." Paper given at the Association of Collegiate Schools of Planning Annual Conference, Minneapolis, MN. 2010.
11 Kenworthy, J./Laube, F.B./Newman, P. *An International Sourcebook of Automobile Dependence in Cities, 1960-1990.* Niwot: University Press of Colorado. 1999.
12 Cervero, R. *The Transit Metropolis: a Global Inquiry.* Washington, DC: Island Press. 1998.
13 Pucher, J./Buehler, R. "Making Cycling Irresistible: Lessons from the Netherlands, Denmark and Germany." In: *Transport Review.* 28. 2008. p. 495–528.

BEYOND THE NETWORKED CITY? SUBURBAN CONSTELLATIONS IN WATER AND SANITATION SYSTEMS

Jochen Monstadt & Sophie Schramm

Water and sanitation systems are critical preconditions for suburbs.[1] These (mostly) "circulatory systems" have enabled the functioning and growth of suburbs importing critical water resources for domestic and commercial uses, by "eliminating" wastes, by protecting the public health and safety, and by helping to control many forms of pollution.[2]

At the same time, due to the global increase in suburban population and economic activity, water and sanitation infrastructures are more and more an outcome of the differentiated suburban spaces. Their presence, functioning and accessibility and the regulatory, operational and user practices constitute indicators of the suburban sustainabilities and qualities of life. The study of water and sanitation systems — sociotechnical infrastructures that involve both material and social components — can thus be regarded as a dynamic key to observing the widespread, but spatially differentiated, phenomena of suburbanization.

It is one characteristic of suburban water and sewage systems (and such networked infrastructures in general) that once they are in place, their physical networks and artifacts, but also their engineering culture and their patterns in the operation, financing, use, and governance become fixed and obdurate.

As a consequence of their physical durability and long investment cycles, existing systems represent remnants of earlier investments, knowledge and planning decisions, the logic of which may no longer apply. Due to the interdependencies and complementarities among the social and physical components of infrastructure systems and their close interrelatedness to their spatial environments, contemporary suburban water and sanitation systems can be locked in to path-dependent technological development trajectories. Accordingly, once they are built, these suburban systems may prove to be annoying obstacles to changes in the morphologies of cities and suburbs and in the economic and political relationships between them.

The objective of this essay is to explore the path dependencies and the recent erosion of persistent sociotechnical paradigms in constructing, operating and renewing suburban water and sanitation systems and the shift towards more diverse constellations of these systems. We argue that the unitary provision of networked water and sanitation services — a key focus of urban reforms in the nineteenth and twentieth centuries — is under increasing pressure due to high costs and economic constraints and also sociotechnical innovations and environmental regulations. At the same time, there is a growing awareness that the low levels of connection to such networked systems of suburbs in the Global South can no longer be regarded as temporary phenomena.[3] Our key hypothesis is that diverse suburban constellations are increasingly challenging and undermining traditional models of unitary networked urbanism. The emergence of more diverse and complex suburban constellations, we argue, offers new opportunities for introducing spatially adapted technological and organizational solutions but also entails risks of splintered (sub)urban landscapes.

The Rise and Pitfalls of Networked Suburbanism in the Global North

As a consequence of population growth in the nineteenth century, cities in Europe and North America undergoing rapid industrialization periodically suffered from epidemic diseases. Following the success of the first modern, centralized sewer system — in 1843 in Hamburg, Germany — prevalent decentralized solutions (e.g., privy vault-cesspool, dry sewage) have been replaced in urban areas in Europe.[4] It became a central issue in urban reform agendas to improve the living conditions of the modern industrial city by overcoming the existing fragmentary and highly localized arrangements in water supply and sanitation by investing heavily in centralized, standardized and municipally controlled sanitation and water networks that cover an entire urban area.

As various scholars in the history of technology and cities have illustrated, one of the most influential ideals to build and manage cities has been that of the "networked city" — and the associated ideals of the "sanitary" or "hydraulic city."[5] Although these paradigms have never fully corresponded with urban realities they have guided urban and infrastructure planning worldwide. Most obviously, these ideals refer to the technological design and morphology of cities integrated and ordered by infrastructure networks covering the entire urban territory. Beyond a centralized topology of technical infrastructures and resource flows defining the city and its territorial boundaries, the modernist urban ideals also refer to a specific organizational model in the operation, use and planning of cities and infrastructures: Firstly, they include the notion of monopolistic water and sewage companies, usually under public ownership, providing for ubiquitous and non-exclusive "public services" to all users at unitary tariffs within an urban territory.[6] Secondly, it entails the notion of passive customers not actively engaged in the production or management of the services. And thirdly, it assumes that the provision of these services is closely attached to, highly regulated and partially funded by the state. Engineers, planners, reformers and public health officials have thus aspired to align with this hegemonic ideal of a "good" or "modern" city[7] in (re)producing cities worldwide.

While initially confined to high-density urban centers, the diffusion of the networked paradigm of urbanism proceeded during the twentieth century across Europe and North America. As neighborhoods and industrial districts spread into the urban hinterland, municipal services were extended to low-density suburban areas.[8] The construction of universal, centralized networks was considered crucial to social and spatial cohesion and pollution control. The transfer of the networked city ideal to suburban spaces (and rural settlements)

Open sewer, Hanoi,
Vietnam (2008)
Source: Sophie Schramm

was supported by massive state and regional funding from the 1950s to the 1970s. This meant there was less incentive to search for more cost-effective alternatives and the standing of networked systems was solidified for the next few decades.

The more it became the unquestioned standard of modernity to equip cities and suburbs with universal and centralized networks, regardless of place-specific settlement densities and demographic conditions, the more infrastructural decisions became marginalized in planning discourses. The supply of infrastructure services was increasingly depoliticized and left to technocratic approaches and became politically, discursively and physically invisible. However, in various suburbs traditionally invisible "working infrastructure"[9] has become quite apparent as a result of the increasingly evident problems of these suburban systems.

The increasing costs to operate, renew, and extend the networked infrastructure in many suburban areas since the 1990s are one important reason. Today, many municipalities are faced with the decay of infrastructure built decades ago, including leakage problems and failure to meet new environmental regulations. Due to shifts from taxpayer-financing to user-financing in most European and North American jurisdictions, investments in maintenance, renewal, and replacement have to be raised within the local water and sanitation districts. This is particularly problematic for suburban areas that are characterized by dispersed development, outward expansions, and leapfrog growth patterns. In these low-density areas, the length of inter-neighborhood networks connecting separated service areas and the overall costs in the operation, maintenance, and renewal of infrastructure are considerably higher than in compact urban areas.[10]

These high costs thus raise questions about affordability and unpopular fee increases in many suburban water and sanitation districts, but also questions of spatial justice. Where urban centers and suburban communities build a common water and sanitation district, urban users end up cross-subsidizing the higher costs of provision in the low-density suburban fringe. Countries such as the US or Canada are expected to experience ongoing population growth, associated with increasing demands for urban land, housing, and infrastructure. In contrast, various European countries but also several regions in the US, will increasingly have to adapt their regional and urban infrastructure to cope with demographic shrinkage. Both demographic growth and shrinkage take place primarily in suburban areas and challenge the network's affordability and flexibility to adapt to fluctuating demands.

However, it is not only the recent reduction of state and regional funding, increasing suburban costs and inflexibility that have put municipalities and utility companies under pressure to search for alternatives. One of the most important reasons is environmental pressures — such as the low efficiency in the supply of drinking water, overexploitation of limited groundwater resources, and the huge costs and energy expenditures in the treatment and transport of water and sewage. Municipalities also face new investment requirements in closing nutrient cycles, saving energy, and generating renewable energy from wastewater, and in reducing the emission of greenhouse gases, micro-pollutants etc.[11]

As a consequence of these trends and the growing competitiveness of alternative technologies, the use of decentralized sanitation and water systems in suburban and, above all, newly urbanizing areas is increasing. Particularly in semi-arid regions, decentralized systems have become increasingly important in the supply of water for drinking, industrial uses, and irrigation and in groundwater replenishment. For example, numerous initiatives in Southern California have invested heavily in the recycling of stormwater (e.g., Santa Monica) or even wastewater (e.g., Orange County) to cope with the increasing costs and regulations associated with drinking water. The urban edges of Northern European cities like Lübeck, Hamburg, Berlin, and Stockholm have seen the installation of decentralized sanitation systems that allow for the reuse of resources, the generation of biogas and localized stormwater percolation.[12] The comparatively rapid and low-density urbanization patterns in North America, coupled with a lack of technical infrastructure investment, make decentralized systems, like septic tanks, an increasingly attractive alternative to centralized systems because of their far cheaper capital, operation, and maintenance costs.[13]

Despite the economic and ecological advantages proven in various studies, these more decentralized approaches are not at all the norm in contemporary suburban spaces in the Global North. Not only do they require overcoming sociotechnical path dependencies —

Roadside flooding in Surabaya,
Indonesia (2011)
Source: Imelda Nurwisah

such as the institutional divide between water and sanitation systems with separate operations, regulatory bodies, persistent engineering cultures, investment and planning models, etc. — but also have to be adjusted to existing settlement structures. However, suburban spaces can thus be regarded as places of diversification in which both established and new "system builders" experiment and test innovative practices beyond the ideal of the networked city.

Subverting Networked Urbanism: Diversification of Suburban Infrastructure in the Global South

Urban areas in the Global South cannot be defined based on the access to centralized networks, but have mostly been fragmented ever since urbanization processes gained speed at the end of the nineteenth century. Networks and urban engineering plans have long focused on the infrastructural needs of colonial elites, with the often unrealized promise of later network extensions to the "majority" population.[14] The modern ideal of a unitary, orderly city, integrated by networked infrastructure, was often remodeled as a system of "spatial apartheid" confined to the communities of the colonial power holders surrounded by non-networked but densely populated settlements.[15]

Also, after independence these diverse constellations in urban infrastructure were only in exceptional cases radically changed, since government bodies have been unable or unwilling to extend centralized infrastructures along with urban growth.[16] Consequently, in many cities in the Global South the ideal of the ubiquitously networked city has only been realized in the formerly colonial urban centers or in wealthy neighborhoods, if at all.[17] In the manifold suburban spaces, diverse and partly fragmented sociotechnical arrangements are often placed in direct neighborhood resulting in a mosaic of networked and non-networked water and sanitation arrangements.

These sociotechnical constellations are closely related to broader dynamics of (re)producing suburban space in the Global South. Commonly among these diverse regions, rapid urbanization under conditions of poverty has given rise to peculiar land and infrastructure development patterns and the emergence of megacities that inhibit the installation of citywide technical networks.[18] In many of these regions, the reproduction of suburban space is shaped by the conditions of informality and self-organization[19] defying the implementation of comprehensive master plans or reliable investments in networked infrastructure.

In many urban regions of the Global South, foreign direct investments flow exclusively into "islands of wealth," suburban residential estates or business districts walled off from their surroundings.[20] Many of the water supply and sanitation infrastructures within these suburban areas can be characterized as "satellite systems," local systems not directly connected to the central networks of the urban core, providing services with relatively high standards to the local populations.[21] Examples of planned suburban developments in Hanoi, Vietnam demonstrate that these systems vary with regards to their technological characteristics.[22]

However, their construction and maintenance is in most cases provided by subsidiaries of investment and building companies instead of public utilities.

These "premium network spaces" are often surrounded by neighboring low-income communities, settlements displaying very different morphological and infrastructural features. These settlements are often constructed through self-organization by local communities under conditions of poverty and lack investments in technical infrastructures from external sources — be it state agencies, public utilities, or the private sector.[23] Consequently, water supply and sewerage is provided by communities or even single households themselves — e.g., by local wells, small water merchants, community standpipes or pit latrines for sanitation.[24]

These constellations of basic service provision can result in drastic social inequalities. Such is the case in the periurban settlements of Nairobi, Kenya, where citizens are forced to buy water at a rate far exceeding the legally stipulated costs for clean water.[25] Additionally, a lack of sanitation options aggravates living conditions in these slum settlements. Other periurban settlements display more functional forms of water and sanitation provision outside direct involvement of public utilities. This is the case in the densely populated periurban settlements of Hanoi, where the maintenance of sewerage lines is managed and implemented by local communities.[26]

These are just some examples of the wide spectrum of such systems in suburban areas of the Global South. Generally, suburban landscapes do not display a sharp divide between centralized and decentralized solutions. Rather, hybrid "mixtures"[27] of networked and non-

Flood control infrastructure
near suburban trailer park,
Los Angeles (2011)
Source: Roger Keil

networked technical components and of the service provision by public utilities and self-organized initiatives are combined in suburban water and sanitation systems. Under these conditions, the extension of a unitary central system into the diverse suburban landscapes not only seems to be an unfeasible "mirage,"[28] but might also conflict with the goal of distributive justice. This is the case in Cape Town, South Africa, where extending uniform water and sanitation to the urban edges and suburban areas threatens to aggravate social injustice, as even subsidized tariffs provided by public utilities exclude the poorest.[29] Still, cross-subsidies might convince wealthier groups to leave the unitary network for local providers more advantageous to them.

And yet, despite the diversity of suburban morphologies and demographics, providing alternative water and sanitation service provision is not a universally applicable solution to discrimination. It is, in fact, subject to the cooperation of state agencies and other influential actors who often have vested interests in the status quo. In the slums of Nairobi, members of local administrations informally tolerate or even promote the vending of water at exploitative costs.[30] In periurban settlements of Dhaka, Bangladesh, public utilities engage in informal activities to extend water and sewerage lines and to negotiate water bills.[31] Such blurring of boundaries of the formal and informal spheres are common in the manifold mosaic (sub)urban landscapes of the Global South, and often undermine a socially just provision of infrastructure services.

Open sewer, Nairobi,
Kenya (2006)
Source: Sophie Schramm

These cases illustrate that decentralized and semi-centralized systems are common in suburban areas throughout the Global South, be it through the buying-in of professional services through private contractors for the economic elites or various forms of self-organization by marginalized urban groups. These diverse forms of infrastructure provision are shaped by (sub-)urbanization processes and perpetuate the plurality of suburban spaces in cities of the Global South.

Conclusion

Various engineering studies of the past few decades have proven numerous advantages of decentralized solutions in water and sewage management, such as their higher cost and resource efficiency, or their flexibility to adapt to dynamic and place-specific suburban conditions. However, in urban areas where prevailing networked systems have functioned relatively well for many decades and thus become invisible, radical shifts seem unlikely. Considering the fixity, the sunk costs, and the invested social interests into these networks as well as their close inter-linkage with the built environment and urban practices, decision-makers have little incentive to battle for functionally advantageous, but cost- and conflict-intensive innovations.

Rather, it is those suburban spaces where unitary networked systems are facing the greatest challenges that are seeing the opening of new avenues for innovation in both the Global South and the Global North. The challenges for unitary networked systems emerge from a combination of factors such as rapid urbanization or de-urbanization and shrinkage, urban conditions of informality, spatial fragmentation, and low investments in decaying infrastructures. In those parts of the Global North, where investments in technical infrastructure systems are traditionally high and pressures on water and sanitation systems from rapid (de)urbanization processes are relatively low, environmental issues as well as prospects of worldwide technology markets are key drivers for the development of alternative systems. The growing markets for such solutions are mostly confined to suburban areas, as the built urban centers are usually locked-in, traditional networked systems.

Paradoxically, it might thus be the suburbs — often portrayed as unsustainable — that serve as incubators for innovation. However, the trend towards more resource-efficient, flexible, and affordable suburban services raises new questions of technological functionality, compatibility with the prevailing centralized systems, and of efficient organizational models to operate a diversity of decentralized systems. It also puts new challenges of sociospatial cohesion and solidarity within urban regions, as well as their governability, on the research and policy agenda.[32]

Critical research is required to assess under which conditions decentralized sociotechnical solutions promoted by progressive engineering communities and accompanied by the rise of micro-finance models provide more affordable and sustainable services to the urban poor — or perpetuate or aggravate sociospatial injustice — and result in fragmented landscapes of "micro-suburbs" that may be spatially proximate, while socially and technically disconnected.

Equally important is further research on the suburban governance and public control of heterogeneous decentralized systems. The ongoing shift towards a more diverse array of service providers in urban peripheries and in-between spaces brings about new challenges for comprehensive planning in metropolitan regions.

Endnotes

1 Much of our thinking on the networked city in this essay has been inspired by the workshop "From Networked to Post-Networked Urbanism" in Autun, France, in Summer 2012. We thank all participants and especially the organizers, Olivier Coutard and Jonathan Rutherford, for stimulating discussions.

2 Melosi, M. *The Sanitary City: Urban Infrastructure in America from Colonial Times to the Present.* John Hopkins University Press: Baltimore. 2008. p. 1. The caveat "mostly" refers to the fact that much suburbanization has historically occurred and is occurring still with non-networked local infrastructures such as wells or on-site septic systems.

3 Gandy, M. "The Bacteriological City and Its Discontents." In: *Historical Medical Geography.* 2006. 34, p. 21.

4 Burian, S. J./ Nix, S. J./Pitt, R. E./Durrans, S. R. "Urban Wastewater Management in the United States: Past, Present, and Future." In: Journal of Urban Technology. 7(3). 2006. p. 33–62.

5 Dupuy, G. *Urban Networks: Network Urbanism.* Techne Press. Amsterdam. 2008; Coutard, O./Rutherford, J. "The Rise of Post-Networked Cities in Europe? Recombining Infrastructural, Ecological and Urban Transformations in Low Carbon Transitions." In: Bulkeley, H./Castan Broto, V./ Hodson, M./ Marvin, S. (eds.): *Cities and Low Carbon Transitions.* London: Routledge. 2011. p. 107–125; Gandy 2006. Op. cit.; Melosi 2008. Op. cit.

6 Pincetl, S. "From the Sanitary City to the Sustainable City: Challenges to Institutionalising Biogenic (Nature's Services) Infrastructure." In: *Local Environment.* 15(1). 2010. p. 43–58.

7 Graham, S./Marvin, S. *Splintering Urbanism. Networked Infrastructures, Technological Mobilities and the Urban Condition.* Routledge, London. 2001; Pincetl 2010, Op. cit.

8 Burian et al. 2000. Op. cit., p. 52.

9 Star, S. L. "The Ethnography of Infrastructure." In: *American Behavioral Scientist.* 43(3). 1999. p. 382.

10 Siedentop, S./Fina, S. "Urban Sprawl beyond Growth: the Effect of Demographic Change on Infrastructure Costs." In: *Flux.* 79-80(1). 2010. p. 90–100.

11 Kluge, T./Scheele, U. "Von dezentralen zu zentralen Systemen und wieder zurück? " In: Moss, T./Naumann, M./Wissen, M. (eds): *Infrastrukturnetze und Raumentwicklung.* München: Oekom Verlag. 2008. p. 143–172.

12 Winblad, U./Simpson-Hébert M. *Ecological Sanitation.* Stockholm: Stockholm Environment Institute. 2004.

13 Burian et al. 2000. op. cit.

14 Graham, S. "Constructing Premium Network Spaces: Reflections on Infrastructure Networks and Contemporary Urban Development." In: *International Journal of Urban and Regional Research.* 24(1). 2000. p. 183–200.

15 Balbo, M. "Urban Planning and the Fragmented City of Developing Countries." In: *Third World Planning Review.* 15(3). 1993. p. 23–35.

16 Zetter, R. "Market Enablement and the Urban Sector." In: Hamza, M./Zetter, R. (eds.): *Market Economy and Urban Change – Impacts in the Developing Word.* London: Earthscan. 2004. p. 1–40.

17 Graham/Marvin 2001, op. cit.

18 UN-Habitat. *State of the World's Cities 2008/2009 – Harmonious Cities.* Nairobi: United Nations Human Settlements Programme. 2008.

19 AlSayyad, N./Roy, A. "Urban Informality: Crossing Borders." In: Roy, A./ AlSayyad, N. (eds.): *Urban Informality. Transnational Perspectives from the Middle East, Latin America and South Asia.* Oxford: Lexington Books. 2004. p. 1–6.

20 Cf. Grant, R./Nijman, J. "Globalization and the Corporate Geography of Cities in the Less-Developed World." In: *Annals of the Association of American Geographers.* 92(2). 2002. p. 320–40.

21 Letema, S./van Vliet, B./van Lier, J. B. "Reconsidering Urban Sewer and Treatment Facilities in East Africa as Interplay of Flows, Networks and Spaces." In: van Vliet, B./Spaargaren, G./Oosterveer, P. (eds): *Social Perspectives on the Sanitation Challenge.* Dordrecht. Springer. 2010. p.145–162.

22 Schramm, S. "Semicentralized Water Supply and Treatment — Options for the Dynamic Urban Region of Hanoi, Vietnam." In: *Journal of Environmental Assessment Policy and Management.* 13(2). 2011. p. 285–314.

23 UN-Habitat. *The Challenge of Slums — Global Report on Human Settlements 2003.* Nairobi. United Nations Human Settlements Programme. 2003.

24 Ibid.

25 Cf. Kariah-Gitau, S./Mitullah, W./Syagga, P. *Nairobi Situation Analysis.* Nairobi: Government of Kenya. United Nations Human Settlements Programme. 2001.

26 Schramm 2011, op. cit.

27 Oosterveer, P./ Spaargaren, G. "Meeting Social Challenges in Developing Sustainable Environmental Infrastructures in East African Cities." In: van Vliet, B./Spaargaren, G./Oosterveer, P. (eds.): *Social Perspectives on the Sanitation Challenge.* Dordrecht. Springer. 2010. p. 11–30.

28 Letema et. al. 2010, op. cit.

29 Jaglin, S. "Differentiating Networked Services in Cape Town: Echoes of splintering urbanism?" In: *Geoforum.* 39(6). 2008. p. 1897–1906.

30 Kariah-Gitau, S. et. al 2001, op. cit.

31 Hossain, S. "Informal Dynamics of a Public Utility: Rationality of the Scene Behind a Screen." In: *Habitat International.* 35. 2001. p. 275–285.

32 Coutard/Rutherford 2011, op. cit.

SUBURBS AT RISK

Robin Bloch,
Nikolaos Papachristodoulou &
Donald Brown

We write as urban development planners and analysts, involved in projects and in applied and academic research. Wherever we work — and notably in Sub-Saharan Africa, South and East Asia and Latin America — we see a new and intensified phase of rapid and large-scale urban population growth and spatial expansion. At the same time, we witness that cities and towns undergoing such growth, particularly in low and middle-income nations, are frequently exposed to a multitude of natural hazards. Indeed, current urban growth patterns appear to have significantly amplified the exposure of urban populations to hazard risks, markedly but not exclusively those broadly characterized as the urban poor.

This short paper provides an overview of how growth and expansion, principally in the form of peripheral suburban land development, exposes varied suburban settlement forms and suburbanisms to disaster and climate change risk. We highlight the growing problem of flooding in this context, and then discuss planning issues and responses.

This is a period of continuing, rapid urbanization, particularly in the Global South. According to the 2011 Revision of the World Urbanization Prospects,[1] the urban population is projected to increase from 3.6 billion in 2011 to 6.3 billion in 2050. The level and speed with which individual countries and individual cities within regions are growing varies. Cities in the developing world are expected to account for 90 percent of urban population growth, of which an 80 percent share will belong to Asia and Africa alone — currently the world's least urbanized regions. Latin America, with a current urbanization level of almost 80 percent, is experiencing a decelerating rate of urban population growth.

Urban population growth will be increasingly concentrated in large cities of one million or more dwellers. The percentage of the world urban population living in these cities is expected to increase from 40 percent in 2011 to 47 percent in 2025. Megacities of 10 million and above are expected to experience the largest population percentage increase among cities with populations of one million or more, as they increase from 9.9 percent in 2011 to 13.6 percent in 2025. Despite the decline in the proportion of people living in smaller urban centers, about 40 percent of the urban population will, in fact, continue to live in cities with less than one million dwellers.[2]

As it occurs, urban development takes place horizontally (peripheral expansion) and/or "vertically" (up slopes). Urbanization is thus accompanied by urban spatial expansion as cities and towns swell and grow outwards and upwards in order to accommodate population increases. The global urban transition needs to be seen as essentially suburban in character. Moreover, urbanization as suburbanization drives local and regional environmental changes, by altering land cover, hydrological systems, and biogeochemistry.[3]

Suburbanization, in fact, is the main reason that urban areas around the world are expanding spatially on average twice as fast than their populations grow. According to Angel et al.,[4] in the twentieth century, average built-up area densities declined and most cities expanded their built-up area more than sixteen-fold. By 2030, the global urban extent is forecasted to increase by 185 percent from the 2000 levels.[5] This is about 1.2 million square kilometers of new urban land, equivalent to an area about the size of South Africa. While expansion will occur in all regions, projections show that the majority of this will take place in the developing world. Almost half of the projected increase will occur in Asia. Africa, though, is projected to experience the highest rate of increase in urban land cover, at 590 percent over the 2000 levels.[6]

Spatial expansion often occurs in hazard-prone areas, such as floodplains, coastal and inland areas, as well as on landslide-prone slopes. Consequently, the exposure of urban populations to natural hazards is increasing. In 2011, 60 percent — or about 890 million people living in cities with one million dwellers or more — were located in areas of high risk of exposure to at least one natural hazard.[7] These can include floods, droughts, tropical storms (e.g. cyclones), heat waves, high winds, extreme cold, and sea-level rise. Many settlements are also located in areas exposed to non-climate related hazards, notably earthquakes, which accounted for the majority of disaster casualties in the past decade.[8]

Disaster statistics show that flood events are growing faster than many other non-climate related hazards including earthquakes, although McGuire[9] argues that earthquakes can be triggered by climate change. In the short-term and for developing countries in particular, the factors affecting exposure to floods are increasing rapidly as urbanization concentrates more people and assets at risk. In the longer term, however, climate change is likely to be one of the most important drivers of future changes in flood risk.[10]

Floods are natural phenomena that become natural disasters when people's lives and/or infrastructure are affected. Flooding, particularly in cities, is a direct cause of massive and widespread devastation, the loss of lives, and economic damages. According to the United Nations International Strategy for Disaster Reduction (UNISDR), more than 150,000 people were killed between 1992 and 2012 by floods. Immediate loss of life from flooding seems to be increasing more slowly or even decreasing over time.[11] However, the numbers of people afflicted by floods, and financial, economic and insured damages, have all increased. In 2010 alone, 178 million people were struck by floods. The total financial losses in exceptional years such as 1998 and 2010 exceeded $40 billion.[12]

Disaster statistics also show that mortality risk for all weather-related hazards remains concentrated in nations with weak governance and low GDP.[13] Flood events, in particular, are becoming more frequent and intense in the cities and towns of developing countries — a trend that is consistent with climate change projections. Floods affect urban settlements of all types — from small villages and mid-sized market towns and service centers, to large cities and metropolitan regions. And as suburbanization has become the defining feature of urban population growth, large-scale spatial expansion is placing new settlement areas at risk, with the exposure of urban populations and infrastructure to hazard risks thus often increasing. Flood risk is no longer an external condition; it is instead a constitutive dimension of the current era of global sub(urbanization).

Energy distribution, Mitchell's
Plain, South Africa (2002)
Source: Roger Keil

Some argue that the impacts of disasters are actually largely under-estimated because they fail to consider "extensive risk," which is associated with the exposure of dispersed population concentrations, particularly in rural, and peripheral suburban and periurban areas, to small disasters of low to moderate intensity, such as localized floods.[14] The impacts of these "small disasters" and "everyday hazards" are too small to be classified as major disasters, which are typically associated with "intensive risks" linked to high intensity hazard events.[15] Yet, "extensive risk" is a main characteristic of suburban areas in cities where unplanned development in floodplains, aging (or non-existent) drainage infrastructures, increased paving and other impermeable surfaces, and a lack of flood risk reduction activities all contribute to the increased impacts of flooding.

It is important to note, however, that there is no direct link between increasing urban populations and increasing disaster risk.[16] Experience from high-income countries and some middle-income countries shows that urban growth and expansion can take place without escalating hazard risks. This is in line with the fact that disaster risk is most times concentrated within low-income populations or within city districts and/or peripheral (suburban) areas with high concentrations of low-income groups in poorer countries. These are often among the most densely populated parts of cities and towns, and/or include informal settlements.[17] Here, swift-paced urban expansion, typically occurring without structured or agreed land use development plans and regulations, makes conditions more difficult.

In addition, the urban poor's exclusion from the formal economy, lack of access to basic services, and inability to afford good quality housing often means a location in dense-

Community Toilet, Mitchell's
Plain, South Africa (2002)
Source: Roger Keil

ly populated, usually peripheral informal settlement areas that are increasingly exposed to flooding. In Dakar, Senegal for example, new and informal settlements on the city's outskirts are regularly affected by flooding. Mombasa, Kenya often experiences coastal flooding that result in damages to settlements and infrastructure, loss of human lives, and increased incidence of waterborne diseases.[18] Rapidly urbanizing cities across Southeast Asia are particularly vulnerable to flash floods associated with tropical storms, which have had devastating impacts for cities such as Bangkok in Thailand in 2011 and Manila in the Philippines in 2012. Urban flood risk is also a common feature of many cities in Latin America where populations are widely concentrated in low-lying coastal areas and steep slopes.

The increasing risks associated with a variety of climate and non-climate related hazards have attracted increasing attention to the important role that urban planning must play in building resilience.

Within this debate, the compact city paradigm is widely proposed as a universally valid planning framework for achieving sustainability. The paradigm is aimed principally at limiting the negative impacts of urban spatial expansion or "sprawl" through planning policies that support compact urban form and urban containment. However, the application of the "compact city" ideal in developing countries is problematic.[19] Compact urban form and high density can actually work to increase urban risk by concentrating more people and assets in hazard-prone areas (e.g., steep slopes and flood plains), and an increase in impermeable surfaces and poor quality construction. The rationale for higher density development

Water leak Zwelihle Township,
South Africa (2002)
Source: Roger Keil

can also overlook overcrowding and congestion, which remain acute planning problems in many cities of the Global South.

A closer examination of urban risk shows, in fact, that sprawl is not the problem, but rather the lack of adequate land use planning and infrastructure provision in rapidly growing and expanding settlements. A useful starting point for reducing vulnerability in the built environment is to consider the two main planning approaches for achieving this objective. The first is the location approach, which seeks to limit development in at risk areas (e.g., through zoning), while the second is the design approach, which permits development in at risk areas, but seeks to control how buildings are designed and constructed (e.g., through the implementation/ enforcement of building codes).[20] Integrated vulnerability and risk mapping and assessments also have particular value for informing planning policies and infrastructure provision relevant to both approaches. These assessments are most effective when they integrate different kinds of information, including past trends and future projections for hazards (including downscaled climate models and scenarios), data on underlying socioeconomic risk factors and spatial analysis of "hot spot" locations or "most vulnerable" populations.[21] Recent experience also suggests that integrating local knowledge and scientific knowledge can lead to more effective policymaking and practice.[22]

Assessments should also be used to inform integrated urban flood (and other disaster) risk management measures that are aligned with land use planning and management. These measures are typically structural or non-structural.[23] Structural measures mainly involve hard-engineering solutions (e.g., drainage channels) aiming at reducing flood risk by controlling the flow of water both within and outside urban areas. They are complementary to non-structural measures, which are primarily aimed at reducing the vulnerability of people and assets through better land use planning and city management. Structural and non-structural measures should be integrated with one another. Indeed, the uncertainty associated with future climate change combined with rapid urbanization may well require that we move away from a traditional reliance on hard-engineered defenses, towards low/no regret non-structural solutions aimed at building adaptive capacity in the short-term. This will require stronger municipal authorities and more cooperative urban governance.[24]

Integrated flood risk management encompasses more than land use planning, and is closely linked to broader urban planning and management policy and practices. Urban flood risk management strategies can be linked with poverty reduction and climate change adaptation initiatives, and with more specific planning issues, including housing provision, land tenure, urban infrastructure delivery, and basic service provision. Integrated solutions can contribute to flood risk reduction, while simultaneously creating opportunities to achieve more sustainable and resilient urban development.[25]

Further elaborating and deploying these approaches and solutions will become more urgent as urbanization as suburbanization intensifies. The suburbs of the future have arrived, but rather than "the death of the soul" J.G. Ballard foresaw in the 1980s, we can witness variety, vitality, movement, and progression — and his drowned world, as new residents confront disaster. This is by far contemporary suburbanization's greatest — and life *and* soul threatening — challenge.

Endnotes

1 United Nations. "*World Urbanization Prospects: The 2011 Revision.*" United Nations Department of Economic and Social Affairs/Population Division. 2012.
2 Ibid.
3 Seto, K. C./Sánchez-Rodríguez, R./Fragkias, M. "The New Geography of Contemporary Urbanization and the Environment." In: *Annual Review of Environment and Resource.* 2010. 35. p. 167–194.
4 Angel, S./Parent, J. /Civco, D.L./ Blei, A.M. *Atlas of Urban Expansion.* Cambridge: Lincoln Institute of Land Policy. 2010. Online at http://www.lincolninst.edu/subcenters/atlas-urban-expansion/.
5 Seto, K. C./Güneralp, B./Hutyra, L. "Global Forecasts of Urban Expansion to 2030 and Direct Impacts on Biodiversity and Carbon Pools." In: *Proceedings of the National Academy of Sciences of the United States of America.* 2012.
6 Ibid.
7 United Nations, 2012. Op. cit.
8 United Nations International Strategy for Disaster Reduction. 2009. "Disasters in Numbers". Available at: http://www.unisdr.org/files/12470_2009disasterfigures.pdf, 25.02.13.
9 McGuire, B. *Waking the Giant: How a Changing Climate Triggers Earthquakes, Tsunamis, and Volcanoes.* Oxford: Oxford University Press. 2012.
10 Jha, A./ Lamond, J./Bloch, R./ Bhattacharya, N./Lopez, A./ Papachristodoulou, N./ Bird, A./ Proverbs, D./ Davies, J./ Barker, R. "Five Feet High and Rising: Cities and Flooding in the 21st Century." Policy Research Working Paper 5648, World Bank, Washington, D.C. 2011. http://tinyurl.com/asgq3ua, 25.02.13.
11 Jha, A./ Bloch, R./Lamond J. "Cities and Flooding: A Guide to Integrated Urban Flood Risk Management for the 21st Century." World Bank, with support by the Global Facility for Disaster Reduction and Recovery. Washington D.C. 2012.
12 Jha/Lamond et. al, 2011. Op. cit.
13 United Nations International Strategy for Disaster Reduction.

"Revealing Risk, Redefining Development: The 2011 Global Assessment Report on Disaster Risk Reduction." Geneva. 2011.
14 Dodman, D./Brown, D./Francis, K./Hardoy, J./Johnson, C./Satterthwaite, D. "Understanding the Nature and Scale of Urban Risk in Low- and Middle-Income Countries and its Implications for Humanitarian Preparedness, Planning and Response". Prepared for DfID. 2013.
15 Ibid.
16 Dodman, D. "Urban Density and Climate Change." Analytical Review of the Interaction between Urban Growth Trends and Environmental Changes Paper 1. United Nations Population Fund: New York. 2009.
17 Ibid.
18 Awuor C./ Orindi, V./ Adwera, A. "Climate Change and Coastal Cities: The case of Mombasa, Kenya." In: *Environment and Urbanization.* b2008. 20(2). p. 231–242.
19 Brown, D. "Challenging the Conceptual boundaries of the Dominant EuroAmerican Compact City Paradigm in sub-Saharan Africa: The Need for Southern Alternatives to Compact Urban Form and High Density." *DPU Working Paper Series.* Forthcoming.
20 Johnson, C. "Creating an Enabling Environment for Reducing Disaster Risk: Recent Experience of Regulatory Frameworks for Land, Planning and Building in Low and Middle-Income Countries." UNISDR Global Assessment Report on Disaster Risk Reduction 2011: Revealing Risk, Redefining Development. Geneva. 2011.
21 Hallegatte, S. et al. "Flood Risks, Climate Change Impacts and Adaptation Benefits in Mumbai: An Initial Assessment of Socio-Economic Consequences of Present and Climate Change Induced Flood Risks and of Possible Adaptation Options." In: OECD Environment Working Papers, No. 27, OECD Publishing. 2010. http://dx.doi.org/10.1787/5km4hv6wb434-en, 25.02.13.
22 Dodman/Francis et. al, 2012. Op. cit.
23 Jha/Lamond et. al, 2011. Op. cit.
24 Ibid.
25 Ibid.

WALKING OUT OF MONTREAL
Roger Keil

His religion and living in this suburb have taught him shame.

It is a lesson he takes on his daily walk to work. He passes the houses of people he does not know, though he has lived on his block for forty-six years.

His walk into the center of the city is a little more than a mile.

D.J. Waldie, *Holy Land. A Suburban Memoir.* New York: St.Martin's Press, 1996: 51.

3

ESSAYS AND IMAGES

SUBURBANIZATION AND THE REMAKING OF METROPOLITAN CANADA

Markus Moos & Pablo Mendez

It is almost dinner time in Canada's third largest metropolitan area, and the streets of Vancouver's central business district are bustling with activity. The rush-hour crowd swells as suburb-bound commuters head to the Skytrain, the region's light-rail transit system. At Waterfront Station, the train burrows underground beneath office towers, fancy shops and tall condominium apartment buildings. The pace of the street life, the concentration of activities, and the availability of public transit in the downtown conform entirely to what we typically think of as "urban."

Once the riders are aboard, the train moves swiftly. Within minutes, it climbs above ground, winding between condominium towers at first but then moving along major roads, sur-rounded largely by single-family homes. Those looking out the rear window of the train see the downtown skyline receding in the distance. The density of the built environment drops quickly as the train moves into the suburbs. Here there are more automobiles, fewer people walking or riding bicycles, and the street life is subdued. This is how we often understood North American suburbs in the past — as a series of low-density, automobile-dependent areas surrounding the downtown. And indeed, suburbs with these characteristics are still being built across the Canadian metropolitan system.

Yet suburbs are also becoming more diverse in built form and social composition. As the Skytrain leaves downtown, passengers sitting up front can see a new set of high-rise developments approaching. They are surrounded by single-family homes and yet further out, another skyline. In the suburban municipalities of Burnaby and New Westminster, people's lifestyles and the built form increasingly resemble those of downtown Vancouver. Growing numbers of high-rise developments are now being built or proposed in suburban areas across metropolitan Canada, sometimes in close proximity to public transit. Not all suburbs are as dispersed as we once imagined them. Central business districts have seen growth as well, but they can no longer be regarded as the sole metropolitan concentrations of residents or employment.

In the *Atlas of Suburbanisms*[1] we have documented these changes across Canada's major metropolitan areas by mapping several characteristics of urban and suburban ways of living,[2] such as the type of buildings we live in, our rates of homeownership and the way we travel to work. We observe that urban ways of living, such as residing

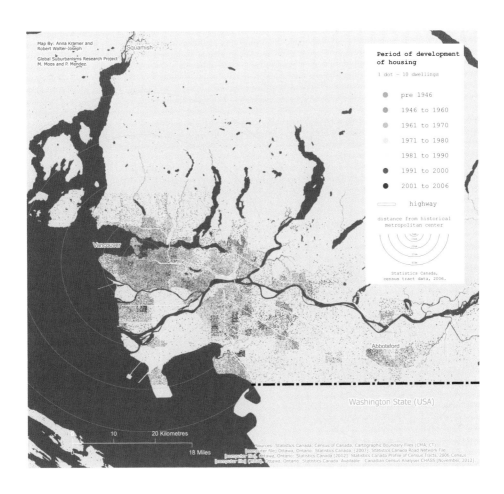

Period of development of the residential housing stock in the Vancouver and Abbotsford metropolitan areas

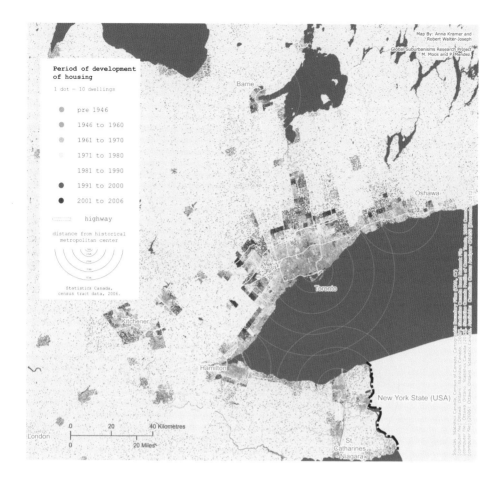

Map By: Anna Kramer and Robert Walter-Joseph

Global Suburbanisms Research Project
M. Moos and P. Mendez

Period of development of housing

1 dot = 10 dwellings

- pre 1946
- 1946 to 1960
- 1961 to 1970
- 1971 to 1980
- 1981 to 1990
- 1991 to 2000
- 2001 to 2006

highway

distance from historical metropolitan center

Statistics Canada, census tract data, 2006.

Barrie

Oshawa

Toronto

Kitchener

Hamilton

London

0   20   40 Kilometres

0   20 Miles

New York State (USA)

St. Catharines
Niagara

in high-rise buildings, increasingly occur in the suburbs but we also found suburban ways of living, such as homeownership and car use, in some central city neighborhoods. The *Atlas* maps reflect an emerging metropolitan structure that is no longer adequately captured, if it ever was, by the two simple categories of the urban and the suburban.

We propose a complementary language of "nodes," "corridors," and "fields" as a way of conceptualizing the emerging metropolitan structure. Conceiving the metropolis as an ensemble of several centers, or nodes, connected by corridors and surrounded by low-density areas, or fields, is not new. It is inspired by a long lineage of urban theorists who have worked with similar ideas, including Jean Gottmann, Stuart Chapin, James Vance, Pierce Lewis, and Paul Knox. The language of nodes and corridors also borrows from the field of urban planning, where the words are used to designate concentrations of activity in and around public transit.[3] Conceptually, these terms have a great deal of potential but this has yet to be fully explored.

Period of development of the residential housing stock in the Greater Toronto Area

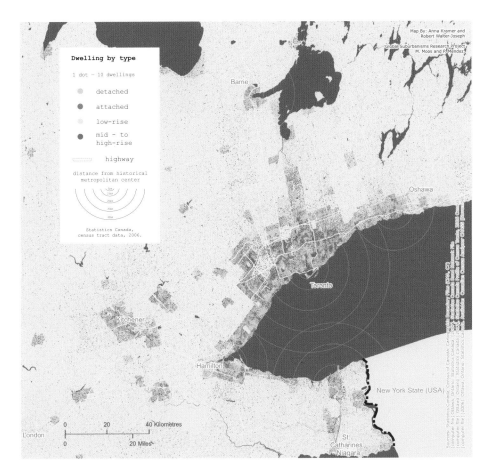

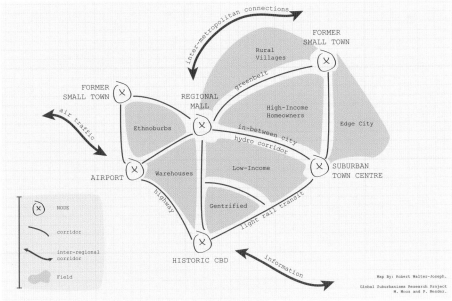

above: Types of residential dwellings in the Greater Toronto Area

below: The urban structure conceptualized as nodes, corridors and fields

Map By: Anna Kramer and
Robert Walter-Joseph

Global Suburbanisms Research Project
M. Moos and P.Mendez

Sources: Statistics Canada, Census of Canada, Cartographic Boundary Files 2006, Ottawa, Ontario, Statistics Canada, [computer file] Ottawa, Ontario, Statistics Canada, [2007]. Ottawa, Ontario, Statistics Canada, [2006]. Ottawa, Ontario, Statistics Canada, [2006]. Available: Canadian Census Analyser CHASS [2012]

**Adults 15+ by
generation of
immigration**

1 dot = 25 persons

● 1st generation

● 2nd generation

● 3rd generation
or more

▭▭▭ highway

distance from historical
metropolitan center

Statistics Canada,
census tract data, 2006.

Barrie

Oshawa

Toronto

Kitchener

Hamilton

New York State (USA)

London

St.
Catharines
Niagara

0   20   40 Kilometres

0   20 Miles

One advantage of using these terms is that they enable us to speak of several competing centers, which can be organized hierarchically in terms of their function, use
or specialization.[4] A good example is provided by regional malls and newly created
suburban town centers, which now rival in many respects the historical central business district. Other nodes are created by the absorption of smaller towns and cities
into an expanding metropolitan region.[5] The terms describe not only our growing
virtual and physical "mobility,"[6] but also the landscapes created by the infrastructure
that facilitates these flows through corridors, including what Sieverts has called the
"in-between city."[7]

Among Canada's largest metropolitan areas, the concepts do a good job of describing well-
established geographical patterns in places like Vancouver and the emerging regional metropolitan structures surrounding Toronto. Residential growth in Montreal remains most
dispersed while most jobs are in the downtown, but even here a series of nodes are now
developing in the suburbs.[8] The multinodal structure becomes less visible in medium-sized

The Greater Toronto Area:
Population by generation of
immigration

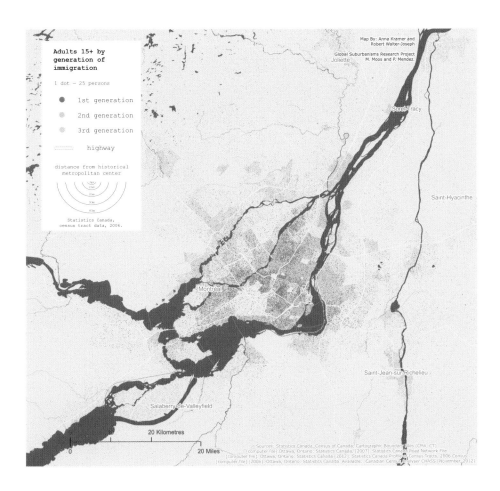

Adults 15+ by
generation of
immigration

1 dot = 25 persons

● 1st generation
● 2nd generation
● 3rd generation

highway

distance from historical
metropolitan center

Statistics Canada,
census tract data, 2006.

Map By: Anna Kramer and
Robert Walter-Joseph

Global Suburbanisms Research Project
M. Moos and P. Mendez

cities where full dispersion creates fields and corridors but few nodes. The structure of nodes, corridors, and fields does not apply equally everywhere.

The conceptualization does recognize that growth continues to take the form of single-family housing at the fringe. The dispersion of people and employment results in several low-density fields, including for instance "edge cities," office parks, or gated communities. The growth of low-density residential fields is also visible in Calgary and Fort McMurray, both of which are deeply connected to Alberta's expanding resource sector. Fields also become characterized by the changes shaping global transformations such as immigration, materializing for instance in so-called ethnoburbs.[9]

Immigration in particular has contributed to the growing ethnic diversity of the suburban population, especially around Toronto (Canada's largest metropolitan area). Montreal, Canada's second largest city, is an exception as its immigrant population remains somewhat more centralized. Nodes, corridors and fields can also be observed at different scales. Nodes, understood as internally complex geographical entities, exist within cities but metropolitan areas themselves

The Montreal metropolitan area:
Population by generation of
immigration

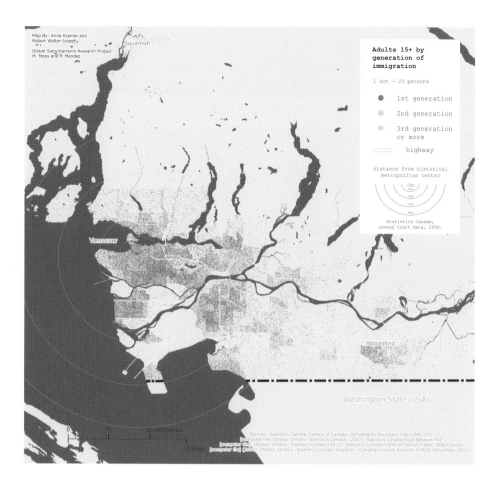

Map By: Anna Kramer and
Robert Walter-Joseph,

Global Suburbanisms Research Project
M. Moos and P. Mendez.

Squamish

Adults 15+ by
generation of
immigration

1 dot = 25 persons

● 1st generation

● 2nd generation

● 3rd generation
or more

highway

distance from historical
metropolitan center

Statistics Canada,
census tract data, 2006.

Vancouver

Abbotsford

Washington State (USA)

become nodes in the networks of national and "global cities," which John Friedmann, Peter Taylor, Manuel Castells, among others, have described. Cities as nodes are linked to each other through transnational corridors of information, shipping, and air traffic. Jean Gottmann already wrote in the 1960s about the awesome spread and interconnections within "megalopolis" — the expansive metropolitan area created by the extension of the suburbs in and around New York City, linking the Eastern Seaboard cities from Boston to Washington, DC.

Today, we are witnessing a global-scale variation on this pattern as metropolitan areas expand their reach virtually through information and financial flows, their interconnectivity increasingly unbounded by physical distance. Vancouver serves again as a notable Canadian example, with its economy and housing market linked to Asian entrepreneurs and capital.[10] Toronto still more so than other Canadian cities is the country's node in global finance flows. Locally, the "megalopolis" therefore takes on a new character. Growth occurs simultaneously in the old downtowns, in dispersed areas, and in new centers, creating networks of nodes that provide a stark contrast to unfettered low-density suburban expansion.

The Vancouver and Abbotsford
metropolitan areas: Population
by generation of immigration

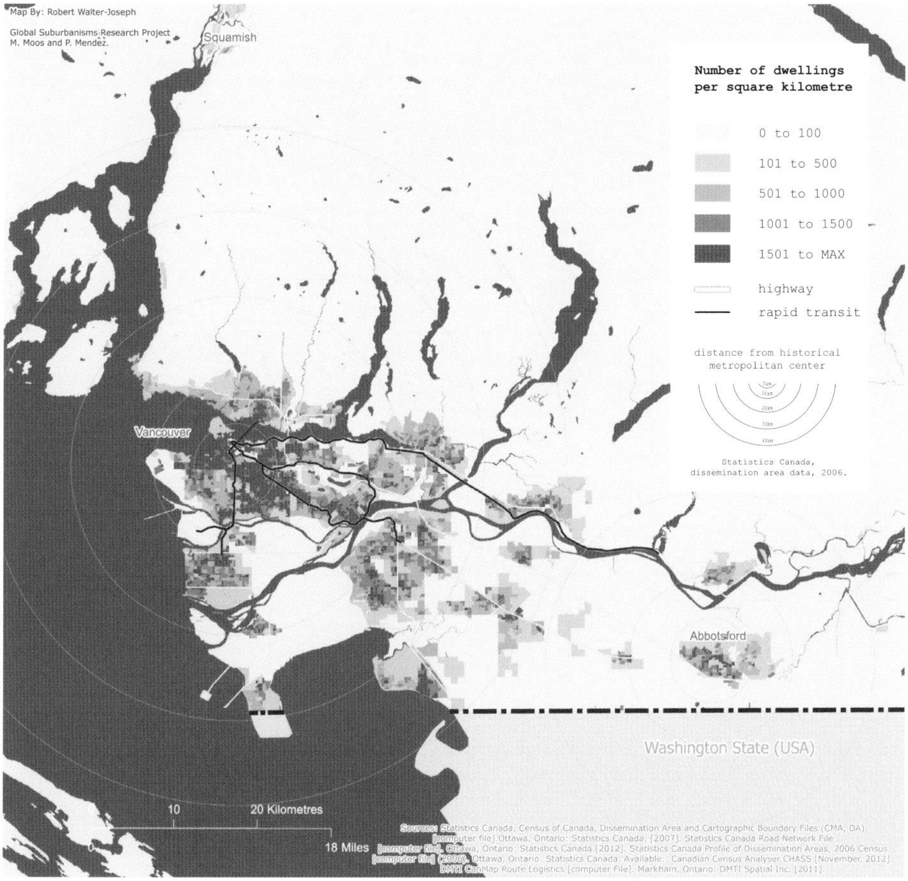
Map By: Robert Walter-Joseph
Global Suburbanisms Research Project
M. Moos and P. Mendez.
Squamish
Number of dwellings per square kilometre
0 to 100
101 to 500
501 to 1000
1001 to 1500
1501 to MAX
highway
rapid transit
distance from historical metropolitan center
Statistics Canada, dissemination area data, 2006.
Vancouver
Abbotsford
Washington State (USA)
10
20 Kilometres
18 Miles
Sources: Statistics Canada, Census of Canada, Dissemination Area and Cartographic Boundary Files (CMA, DA) [computer file] Ottawa, Ontario: Statistics Canada, [2007]. Statistics Canada Road Network File [computer file]. Ottawa, Ontario: Statistics Canada [2012]. Statistics Canada Profile of Dissemination Areas, 2006 Census [computer file] (2006). Ottawa, Ontario: Statistics Canada. Available: Canadian Census Analyser CHASS [November, 2012]. DMTI CanMap Route Logistics [computer File]. Markham, Ontario: DMTI Spatial Inc. [2011].

This emerging structure is in some cases a planned one.[11] Growth management and transportation planning have for some time advocated for the arrangement of land uses into nodes and corridors for efficiency and environmental reasons.[12] This is particularly visible in Vancouver where regional planning has designated specific growth centers and transit corridors, and constrained sprawl using a growth boundary. The Greater Toronto Area, in Ontario, is beginning to see similar patterns with the implementation of the province's Places to Grow plan. More generally, the clustering into nodes was also facilitated by a process of economic restructuring and associated cultural turn that led to growing demand for consuming urban amenities among young artists and then professionals. These dynamics continue, driven by what David Ley has called the "new middle class" and what Richard Florida now refers to as the "creative class." A concurrent process of dispersion into fields is likely a path-dependent effect of postwar housing and transportation policies, assisted by the rising value of land in downtowns.[13] But certainly economic forces and technological change must also be playing a role. Technology can enable dispersion, but the new economy

Dwelling densities in the Vancouver and Abbotsford metropolitan areas

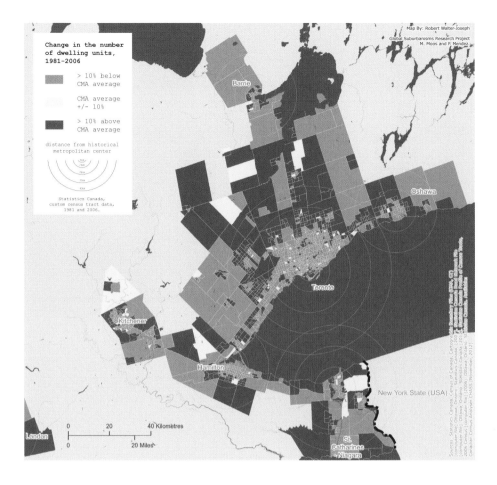

and the creative class increasingly benefit from proximity.[14] The tension between these two opposing forces, it is argued, produces a hierarchy of clusters, or nodes, situated within a broader landscape of otherwise dispersed activities, or fields.[15]

Examination of the Canadian case reveals a clear dual pattern of growth in central city and suburban areas. In recent years, particularly in the first half of the 2000s when credit was more abundant, residential development occurred through the development of high-rise condominium towers in the centers and the continuing expansion of low-density neighborhoods — although multiunit buildings are becoming more common in those areas, too.[16] Moreover, the geography of population growth has increasingly tied smaller towns and cities to the metropolitan structure. Similar dynamics have been documented elsewhere. But Canada is in many ways unique. The scale and characteristics of the nation's immigration flows have played an important role in metropolitan expansion. Economically, cities are increasingly reliant on service sector functions but nationally the resource sector remains omnipotent.

Growth in residential dwelling
units in the Greater Toronto Area

Nodes, corridors, and fields are more clearly manifest in some Canadian metropolitan areas than others. Vancouver, for instance, is somewhat unique in the way the Skytrain so distinctly connects the center and several suburban nodes. But in general, these three concepts seem broadly applicable across the metropolitan landscape of Canada, and perhaps even beyond. We know for example that cities around the world are witnessing a rising concentration of economic and social activity, and that connectivity is increasing between these nodes. At the same time, most growth is now taking place in low-density fields surrounding these areas. The explanatory potential of "nodes," "corridors," and "fields" in the Canadian and other national and transnational contexts begs further exploration. We hope that others will join us in this endeavor.[17]

Growth in residential dwelling units in the Montreal metropolitan area

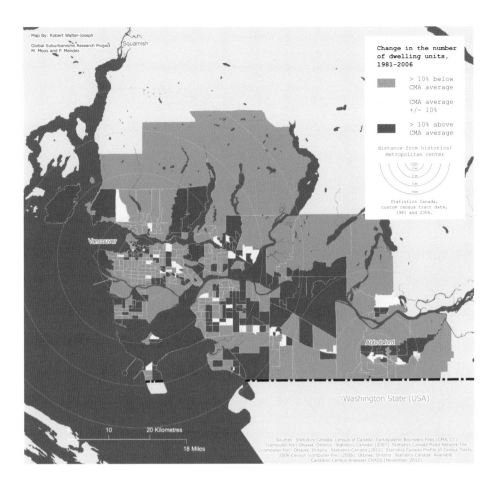

Map By: Robert Walter-Joseph

Global Suburbanisms Research Project
M. Moos and P. Mendez.

Squamish

**Change in the number
of dwelling units,
1981-2006**

> 10% below
CMA average

CMA average
+/- 10%

> 10% above
CMA average

distance from historical
metropolitan center

Statistics Canada,
custom census tract data,
1981 and 2006.

Vancouver

Abbotsford

Washington State (USA)

10   20 Kilometres

18 Miles

Sources: Statistics Canada, Census of Canada, Cartographic Boundary Files (CMA, CT)
[computer file]. Ottawa, Ontario: Statistics Canada [2007]. Statistics Canada Road Network File
[computer file]. Ottawa, Ontario: Statistics Canada [2012]. Statistics Canada Profile of Census Tracts,
2006 Census [computer file] (2006). Ottawa, Ontario: Statistics Canada. Available:
Canadian Census Analyser, CHASS [November, 2012].

Growth in residential dwelling
units in the Vancouver and
Abbotsford metropolitan areas

Endnotes

1   Moos, M./Kramer, A. *Atlas Of Suburbanisms.* 2012. http://env-blogs. uwaterloo.ca/atlas.

2   Walks, A. "Suburbanism as a Way of Life, Slight Return." In: *Urban Studies.* 2012. DOI: 10.1177/0042098012462610.

3   Filion, P. "The Mixed Success of Nodes as a Smart Growth Planning Policy." In: *Environment and Planning B: Planning and Design.* 36 (3). 2009. p. 505–521.

4   Anas, A./Arnott, R./Small, K. "Urban Spatial Structure" In: *Journal of Economic Literature.* 36. 1998. p. 1426–1464.

5   Lang, R./Knox, P. "The New Metropolis: Rethinking Megalopolis." In: *Regional Studies.* 43(6). 2009. p. 789–802.

6   Urry, J. *Mobilities.* Malden: Polity. 2007.

7   Young, D./Keil, R. "Reconnecting the Disconnected: The Politics of Infrastructure in the In-Between City." In: *Cities.* 27(2). 2010. p. 87–95.

8   Shearmur, R./Coffey, W. "A Tale of Four Cities: Intrametropolitan Employment Distribution in Toronto, Montreal, Vancouver and Ottawa-Hull, 1981-2006." *Environment and Planning A.* 34(4). 2002. p. 575–598.

9   Li, W. *Ethnoburb: The New Ethnic Community in Urban America.* Honolulu: University of Hawaii Press. 2009.

10 Barnes. T. et al. "Vancouver: Restructuring Narratives in the Transnational Metropolis." In: Bourne, L. et al. (eds.): *Canadian Urban Regions. Trajectories of Growth and Change.* Toronto: Oxford University Press. 2011.

11 Hall, P. *Cities of Tomorrow: an Intellectual History of Urban Planning and Design in the Twentieth Century.* Oxford: Blackwell Publishers. 1996.

12 Newman, P. and Kenworthy, J. *Sustainability and Cities: Overcoming Automobile Dependence.* Washington, DC: Island Press. 1999.

13 Blais, P. *Perverse Cities: Hidden Subsidies, Wonky Policy, and Urban Sprawl.* Vancouver: UBC Press. 2010.

14 Moos, M./Skaburskis, A. "Workplace Restructuring and Urban Form: The Changing National Settlement Patterns of the Canadian Workforce." In: *Journal of Urban Affairs.* 32(1). 2010. p. 25–53.

15 Audirac, I. "Information Technology and Urban Form." In: *Journal of Planning Literature.* 17(2). 2002. p. 212–226.

16 Grant, J./Filion, P. "Emerging Urban Forms in the Canadian City." In: Filion, P./Bunting, T./Walker, R. (eds.): *Canadian Cities in Transition* (Fourth Edition). Don Mills: Oxford University Press. 2010. p. 307–324.

17 Additional maps and analysis are available on-line at the Atlas of Suburbanisms website. http://env-blogs.uwaterloo.ca/atlas/. Maps by Anna Kramer and Robert Walter-Joseph using Statistics Canada census data.

HIGHRISE

Katerina Cizek

The world's cities are growing fastest at their edges: the fringes, the suburbs. Yet "the suburb" is misunderstood, misrepresented in popular culture, and largely overlooked by politicians and the media. This is a global phenomenon and is not happening "downtown". "The suburb is the most dynamic and problematic part of our city" says Roger Keil.

Source: Paramita Nath.
Courtesy of the National
Film Board of Canada

HIGHRISE is an ongoing project at the National Film Board of Canada. It's a multimedia documentary project about the human experience in vertical suburbs. The project partners with Keil and his team of more than fifty researchers around the world.

The following photographs are from the first major global web-documentary released out of HIGHRISE. Called *Out My Window*, it uses cutting-edge 360° technology to portray the lives of thirteen high-rise residents from thirteen cities around the globe.

Source: Courtesy of the National Film Board of Canada

South City is a huge high-rise suburb twenty kilometers south of Prague in the Czech Republic, with 85,000 residents. Sylva Francova has lived there most of her life. She first moved into the newly built complex, one of the largest concrete buildings in the country, when she was five years old.

Source: Sylva Francova.
Courtesy of the National
Film Board of Canada

Source: Jan Krhovsky.
Courtesy of the National
Film Board of Canada

"We lived on the top floor, the eleventh floor, I realized many years later it was nicknamed 'The Great Wall of China,'" she recalls, "They renovated it a few years ago, it's very colorful, it's now blue and yellow with red balconies. It's a symbol of the South City."

"The government is making sure [South City] doesn't turn into a slum. They are investing in renovations, playgrounds and activities for people," says Sylva, who is now raising her own family here.

The revitalization project in South City includes energy retrofits of the buildings, good public transit links to downtown, and encouraging commercial, social and community activity on site.

"People who live in downtown Prague say that they could never live in the suburban apartment neighborhoods. But for the people who live in the apartments, for us, it's great, and we would never go back downtown. Living in an apartment on the periphery has its benefits. We can walk to the woods, do lots of outdoor sports. That doesn't exist in the center," says Sylva.

Source: Jan Krhovsky.
Courtesy of the National
Film Board of Canada

On the other side of the world, in another suburban apartment neighborhood, fifteen kilometers east of Havana, Cuba, Alamar, the largest public housing project in the world. The lack of proper water and sewage systems is just one of the major environmental and health issues facing the residents living in the crumbling, concrete buildings.

> "There's a lot of contamination, as the pipes were poorly built, says David, "these buildings were built by prisoners, in the sixties, during the Cuban Revolution for the 'New Man.'"

Source: Lazaro Saavedra.
Courtesy of the National
Film Board of Canada

Source: Lazaro Saavedra.
Courtesy of the National
Film Board of Canada

"I wish they'd invent a way to stop the drain from dumping human waste into the ocean. A lot of people swim in there!" says David, who moved here to start a family.

But Alamar has an appeal both culturally and socially. "People participate, and new things form here," says David, a musician and performance artist, pictured playing the guitar. Significantly, Alamar was the birthplace of the Cuban Hip Hop movement. It's a place where self-organization fills in where much of everything else fails.

Source: Lazaro Saavedra.
Courtesy of the National
Film Board of Canada

Source: Reinier Nande Perez.
Courtesy of the National Film
Board of Canada

In Bangalore, India, the high-rise suburban trend is much newer. Springing out of the Information Technology (IT) economic boom, massive gated high-rise communities and Special Economic Zones (SEZs) have popped up around the peripheries of the old town of Bangalore. The SEZs are high security areas, with minimal financial regulation, intended to attract foreign investment.

Source: Paramita Nath.
Courtesy of the National
Film Board of Canada

Source: Paramita Nath.
Courtesy of the National
Film Board of Canada

Yet the IT sector only represents approximately 8 percent of the employment in Bangalore. The rest are mostly low-paid service jobs catering to that 8 percent. For example, Vishwarama is a laundry woman who provides services to IT workers in the garage of a gated high-rise building. Her wages have not risen since her last job, doing the same work, at a hospital just down the road.

Meanwhile, the global recession has hit hard.

"Along this road, there are 3,500 to 4,000 apartments along a three- to four-kilometer stretch in mid-construction", says Abhishek, a resident in one of the completed building complexes nearby.

"All the builders have stopped because of the recession. They have run out of money because of steel prices and concrete prices."

Source: Paramita Nath.
Courtesy of the National
Film Board of Canada

And in Tainan, Taiwan, high-rise buildings on the urban peripheries are built to house the dead. Called *columbaria*, these "homes for the afterlife" each contain thousands of niches for the ashes of the deceased.

> "In the future, as more and more people die, graveyards are going to overflow. But *columbaria* won't let this happen," says Xu, whose 91-year old mother XuLao, already has her niche reserved.

XuLao has consolidated all her relatives here into hundreds of niches. "I want to be together with my children, that's why I paid $5,000 (USD) for this spot," she says.

Concrete high-rise buildings are one of the most commonly built forms of the last century. They are to be found on the peripheries of cities, and on the peripheries of our cultural and political attention. Yet what happens inside is as diverse and complex as human life itself. For more stories from within the towers of glass and concrete, visit the 360º web-documentary at http://high-rise.nfb.ca/outmywindow

HIGHRISE explores vertical living in the global suburbs. It's a multimedia collaborative documentary experiment at the National Film Board of Canada, directed by Katerina Cizek and produced by Gerry Flahive. Over several years, HIGHRISE is generating many projects, including mixed media, interactive documentaries, mobile productions, live presentations, installations and films. Collectively, the projects will both shape and realize the HIGHRISE vision: to see how the documentary process can drive and participate in social innovation rather than just to document it; and to help reinvent what it means to be an urban species in the twenty-first century.

Source: Sylva Francova.
Courtesy of the National
Film Board of Canada

A CITY OF RIVERS AND BROKEN SIDE MIRRORS

Nathan Schaffer

Empty road pulling through a tunnel.

Narrow, what a great word.

Structural symmetry and difference in detail.
Bare feet and smile-lines. Dirty fingernails and
an uneven gait. Pass storefronts and worn-out
signs, soaking up the salt and the dust in the
air. Patterns in pavement cracks,
fingers,
        rivers,
                miles and miles.

Street Music, Marseille (2012)
Source: Nathan Schaffer

MAKING THEM TALK, THEN ACT, TOGETHER! THE GREATER TORONTO SUBURBAN WORKING GROUP

Sean Hertel & Roger Keil

Suburbanization appears often as an inevitable structural process, a wave, an unstoppable growth somehow pushed by an anonymous dynamic. Whether we subscribe to the view that suburbanization is supplied by a ravenous capital accumulation process or demanded by rational market choices by individuals, rarely do we hear the word "sprawl" without its twin, "unplanned." Yet, suburbs are planned, built, financed, and ultimately lived in by many. Who, then, builds the suburbs? That is the question with which we started out.

The Greater Toronto Suburban Working Group or GTSWG — and we are always open to a name change — was established in the Summer of 2010 as a forum for a diverse and expert group of actors and critical observers in suburb-building to share information and work towards innovating new forms of suburban governance in both the inner and outer peripheries of Toronto. We have come to call this region the Greater Golden Horseshoe or GGH: a far-reaching pattern of settlement forming a "horseshoe" shape around the northwestern shoreline of Lake Ontario from the Niagara Escarpment in the west across the Oak Ridges Moraine to the doorstep of the Kawartha Lakes cottage country in the east.

There are many problem constellations that are a part of, and are connected to, our work. The suburbs have become, like the city centers before them, the new arenas for forming and contesting politics, modes of governance, ways of life, and the forms and notions of community. These phenomena manifest themselves in different ways, and at different scales. For example: a shift in municipal governance towards a more suburban sensibility, as the 2010 City of Toronto elections clearly have shown; a growing awareness and organization by residents around issues such as power generation and transmission; and continuing economic and cultural diversification. Even the designations of municipalities are changing quickly in line with the exploding suburbs: our partner, the Town of Markham, has since taken on the designation of City!

We wanted to bring together a group of experts from a variety of disciplines in the suburban governance arena who are actively engaged in the very processes and contexts we wanted to study through our research. The terms of reference for such innovative collaboration were built on a few first principles, and aided by large doses of emphatic belief in the power of deliberative interaction. These were some of our original thoughts:

Collaboration within and across government and non-government actors within the planning and development arena of the GGH is not without precedent. Over the past two

GTSWG Meeting,
United Way York Region,
September 18, 2012
Source: Roger Keil

GTSWG Meeting,
United Way York Region,
September 18, 2012
Source: Roger Keil

decades there have been examples at both macro (e.g., province and regional) and micro (e.g., town or city) scales; confronting specific goals or problems, generating discussion, exchanging information, and making recommendations on existing and proposed policies and programs. This institutional history developed in connection with particular issues or problem constellations.[1]

Macro level collaboration typically includes state-sponsored or state actors such as provincial bodies and/or initiatives, but also provincial-federal arrangements such as joint Royal Commissions, including Waterfront Toronto. Several examples of inter- and intra-regional collaboration have been initiated (and have since come to conclusion) within the GGH in recent years to confront issues of increasing and interconnected complexity. Attempts to address governance, urban sprawl, and the natural environment, for example, have given rise to the Greater Toronto Services Board, Smart Growth Panels, and the Oak Ridges Moraine Tri-Regional Strategy, respectively. It also includes institutional actors and representatives of organized social and economic interests, such as BILD on the side of property capital and the building industry, and environmental organizations, such as STORM or the Greenbelt Alliance, on the side of civic organizations.

Micro-level collaboration is nested within, and often intersects with, collaborative processes and actors at the macro level. The formulation of land use planning policies through comprehensive public and agency consultation processes is an excellent example. Ongoing and recently concluded planning consultations to bring municipal official plans into conformity with the 2006 Provincial Growth Plan for the Greater Golden Horseshoe (e.g., Vaughan and Mississauga) are timely examples of this type of consultation. Another excellent example of micro-level collaboration (non-statutory) are the Advisory Groups struck by the then Town of Markham to provide community-based advice to council on land use policy formulation and development approvals for the smart growth communities of Markham Centre and Cornell.

Intermediary roles are often played by professional organizations such as planning firms, architectural associations, planning organizations, and the like, who may appear on both sides of some planning related arguments and suburbanization projects. As we later explain, this creates a rich environment for the discourse and collaborative action. Collaboration, communication, and capacity-building have become important pillars for contemporary planning theory and practice. There are procedural and substantive aspects to these emerging movements, as claims for more democratic processes have been associated with new political actors and policy arenas (e.g., the environment, culture, identity, etc.). For example, increasing non-professional involvement within (and against) planning and larger urbanization processes over the past few decades has been characterized by planning theorists as a "bottom-up" approach. In this mode, which has been categorized by Friedmann as "social mobilization," interventions in public policy have become increasingly collaborative and community-driven.[2] Another dimension to more recent articulations of the public interest

GTSWG Meeting, Markham
Civic Centre, April 26, 2011
Source: Roger Keil

and associated interventions in public policy is the focus on people's "stories" rather than "problems."[3] This has engendered a "communicative turn" in planning theory; wherein public actions are increasingly influenced through communication among and between actors.[4] The increasing practice and value of "bottom-up" collaborative communication creates an opportunity to explore ways to confront, understand, and intervene in the governance of the GGH suburbs. So, enter our collaborators-partners: Building Industry and Land Development Association (BILD); Canadian Urban Institute; planning and urban design firm DIALOG; Friends of the Greenbelt Foundation; planning and development management firm R.G. Richards and Associates; the City of Markham; The Neptis Foundation; United Way of York Region; and planning and urban design firm Urban Strategies Inc. The coming together of these nine partner-participants has created a very rich and dynamic medium for the discourse; ideal for the percolation, convergence and dissemination of unique experiences and knowledges.

While there have been several examples of collaboration in GGH, rarely has there been collective action across the suburban expanse, specifically.

Examples of previous forms of collaboration within the Toronto suburban governance arena trace their origins to provincial legislation, related bodies, and, in the case of Waterfront Toronto, a joint provincial-federal arrangement.

But the GTSWG is different, of course, in many respects. First of all, the group is not a product of any government or agency-led initiative. That is to say that the GTSWG is a bottom-up, rather than a top-down model. Second, the group is voluntary. Each organization is participating on their own accord (and without compensation for their time and resources) because they are interested in the research we are undertaking. A third is that the GTSWG is aimed at governance itself, and not a product of it. In a kind of ironic twist, the GTSWG is a collaborative apparatus (we hesitate to use the word "structure," although it may very well be one) to inform the way in which other such groups could be formed to

better align the instruments of suburban governance with the challenges and opportunities that suburbanization in the twenty-first century brings.

With a field of study and partners, now what?

Basic terms of reference for our group were drafted in time for our first meeting in the Fall of 2010 at York University. They set out who we are, what we wanted to do, how we could

GTSWG Meeting, Markham
Civic Centre, April 26, 2011
Source: Roger Keil

GTSWG Meeting, Friends
of the Greenbelt Foundation,
February 13, 2012
Source: Roger Keil

GTSWG Meeting, Friends
of the Greenbelt Foundation,
February 13, 2012
Source: Roger Keil

best go about doing that, and what we thought our individual roles and responsibilities should be. For example, each partner organization will host at least one meeting over the three-year term of the group, and share reflections on their work and contribute ideas with the other partners. Important themes to explore together also emerged from the outset, which included the natural environment, land use planning and development, and transportation.

An important undercurrent to the terms was striving towards new ways of defining, and beginning to solve, old and mounting challenges. While sprawl, resource depletion, and congestion continue to dominate most suburban discourses, we are increasingly turning our attention to issues that include: an aging population (and retrofitting communities in response); rapid ethno-cultural diversification (including the rise of "ethnoburbs"); and the increasing demands and complexity of social services.

Though we didn't specifically ask the question, "How can we expect different results unless we adopt different approaches to suburban governance?" this has become a recurring theme in our work. The social and economic composition and structures of our region are changing dramatically, yet the ways we govern and view the region have really not changed much at all.

The terms of reference were also an opportunity to spell out what "governance" and "collaboration" meant to us for the purpose of moving forward in our suburban research. The term "suburb," too, proved to be something requiring a little explanation. Even before we started to meet as a group, we quickly came to realize the subjectivity and jargon in the language many used to describe our field of study.

A purpose-written paper by Ekers, Hamel, and Keil, "Governing Suburbia: Modalities and Mechanisms of Suburban Governance," was prepared to serve as a kind of conceptual road map for the GTSWG; assisting the members to identify and navigate the many phenomena of suburban governance, including providing a definition of "suburb." Reviewing a first draft of this paper at our inaugural meeting provided a solid theoretical framework from which to move. The paper defined a suburban governance terrain that can be described has having three distinct yet overlapping forces or "modalities": the state (e.g., government land controls and infrastructure financing); the market (e.g., private landowners develop land for profit); and private authoritarianism (e.g., privately-financed and controlled infrastructure, including complete "gated communities"). And there are many myths and prejudices associated with "the suburb" and "suburbanization." In reply, the paper defines suburbanization "as the combination of non-central population and economic growth with urban spatial expansion."[5]

So, there we were: a dozen or so academics, planners, designers, developers, geographers and community organizers sitting around a bank of tables at our first meeting together in September 2010, thinking, "now what?" Over two years and nine meetings later we can still ask ourselves that question, to be honest, but the answer is, "quite a bit, actually."

We have completed our "show and tell" phase over this period and have learned much from each other. And whether we realize it or not, we have created much knowledge (and, as we'll say later, the real work is getting that knowledge out into the world and using it to refine and perhaps even create new forms of suburban governance). We have covered a wide array of topics and issues over the course of our meetings so far. We have shared information and experiences about planning and intensification in the suburbs. We have looked at social diversity through the eyes of an architect and heard from the United Way about the challenges of identifying and addressing community needs. We learned about the economic and environmental importance of the Greenbelt. We saw just how vast and complex the region is by learning how spatial information can be better developed and shared to inform decision-making.

We are now in the process of shifting our attention and energy towards packaging what we've learned into a call to action for new ways of seeing and shaping the Greater Golden Horseshoe. We've accomplished much by simply creating a space for this kind of collaboration; by bringing together a diverse group of experts who, under normal circumstances, would not have this kind of opportunity to collaborate. Borrowing from Marshall McLuhan, you could say that our "process is the product." But we acknowledge we still need to go further to translate knowledge from our unique perspectives and shared experiences into action.

What we are working on now is something that we playfully call our manifesto — our ideas, questions and suggested strategies for governing our region in the face of increasingly complex challenges. Part of this manifesto will be an invitation, we think, to transplant our collaborative model to other jurisdictions facing similar challenges. While we acknowledge that suburbs are universal — found in virtually every corner of the urbanized world — they have qualities and circumstances that are uniquely their own.[6] Applying a model of collaboration similar to the one we created through the GTSWG could be a way to better identify and harness the qualities of other suburban regions to forge new ways of seeing and governing those places.

Endnotes

1   On the history of regional governance in southern Ontario, see, for example: Frisken, F. *The Public Metropolis: The Political Dynamics of Urban Expansion in the Toronto Region, 1924-2003.* Toronto: Canadian Scholars' Press Inc. 2008. or Boudreau, J./Hamel, P./Jouve, B./Keil, R. "New State Spaces in Canada: Metropolitanization in Montreal and Toronto Compared." In: *Urban Geography.* 28(1). 2007. p. 30–53.

2   Friedmann, J. *Planning in the Public Domain: From Knowledge to Action.* Princeton: Princeton University Press. 1987.

3   Forester, J. *The Deliberative Practitioner.* Cambridge: MIT Press. 1999

4   See for example Healy, P. "The Communicative Turn on Planning Theory and its Implications for Spatial Strategy Theory." In: Campbell, S./Fainstein S.S. (eds.), *Readings in Planning Theory.* Malden: Blackwell Publishing Ltd. 2003. p. 237–261 or Innes, J. E. "Information in Communicative Planning." In: *Journal of the American Planning Association.* 10(3). 1998. p. 195–200.

5   Ekers, M./Hamel, P./Keil,R. "Governing Suburbia: Modalities and Mechanisms of Suburban Governance." In: Regional Studies. 46(3). 2012. p. 407.

6   Keil, R. "Global Suburbanization: The Challenge of Researching Cities in the 21st Century."In: Logan. S./Marchessault, J./ Prokopow, M. (eds.): *Public 43 (Spring), Suburbs: Dwelling In Transition.* 2011. p. 55–61.

KHODINSKOE FIELD DEVELOPMENT, MOSCOW

ogino:knauss

Re:centering periphery is a documentary project developed by the ogino:knauss collective using different media and formats. The project investigates the contribution of modernist ideology to current global trends of urbanization, with a particular analytical focus on center-periphery relations and how everyday life practices subvert and reinvent suburban spatial-political configurations.

Dom Novogo Byta, shot in Moscow, is the second film of the series. The film starts with the scant remnants of the revolutionary visions created by constructivist architects, who sought communitarian housing solutions to cross the imagined urban landscapes proposed by Soviet propaganda. Finally, it gets lost in the indistinct and monotonous peripheral settlements of high-rises which constitute the undisputed response to the dwelling problem in Russia.

As an emblematic outcome of Moscow's recent urban development, the film closes on an odd mix of abandoned military facilities and emerging gated communities.

Khodinskoe is an ex-military airport inside Moscow which, since the end of the 1990s, has been redeveloped as a residential settlement. The project foresees a park and public facilities, but only massive housing complexes have been realized so far. These are gated communities for wealthy residents surrounding a huge terrain vague divided by the old airfield runaway. The inherently military design of the area is not challenged by the new project. The fenced and hardly accessible environment is preserved and nested, with surreal effect, in the urban fabric.

The new Moscow Central
Business District (2008)

From Re:centering
Periphery #2 – Moscow,
documentary project by
ogino:knauss

(Manuela Conti, Lorenzo Tripodi,
Francesca Mizzoni, Laura Colini)
http://www.oginoknauss.org/
blog/

Khodinskoe field development
site (2010)

ogino:knauss is a collective of
architects and artists dealing
with urban exploration and

innovative representation
forms based in Berlin.

Source: Manuela Conti

FORT MCMURRAY, THE SUBURB AT THE END OF THE HIGHWAY

Claire Major

Fort McMurrray, Alberta is quite literally the crossroads to nowhere, very nearly the terminus of the 400-plus kilometer roadway from north of Edmonton, the provincial capital.[1] It straddles Highway 63, a winter road until the mid-1960s, which remained unpaved until the mid-1970s and now exists, with the exception of a 32-kilometer stretch of its 200-plus kilometer length, as a single lane highway. "Pray for me, I drive 63," a local saying, is no joke given that there were forty-six traffic fatalities between 2008 and the spring of 2012.[2] The highway connects commuters to elsewhere in Alberta, or across the country from British Columbia to Manitoba, transports restless McMurrayites to the siren call of the West Edmonton Mall, putting drivers in a frustrating convoy with slow-moving, wide-load, industrial-scale equipment. Highway 63 cuts through the center of the city — calls for a ring road go unheeded — and with just one public bridge over the Athabasca River, a stalled truck can mean an eight-kilometer trip from downtown to uptown can take ninety minutes. Still, it is the heart of the oil sands, the terrestrial pipeline of people.

What is the link between Fort McMurray as a place to work and as a place to live? Ekers et al. argue that one of the means through which the state governs processes of suburbanization "is through the development of infrastructure and the promotion of mobility as a central value of modernity."[3]

Residential area expansion
(2011)
Source: Claire Major

Oil enables mobility. Is "one road in, one road out" the lifeline of mobility (unless you count off-road vehicles, of which there are plenty in Fort McMurray)? Is a "bridge to nowhere" — the Peter Lougheed Bridge, built in the 1980s, leading to nowhere until Suncor and Shell developed sites over and beyond it — suggestive of such a promotion? Is it enough that people don't just live in houses but that they go to work and drive a vehicle as big as one?[4]

It is so modern, so mobile that another town entirely — 39,271 people according to the 2012 municipal census — exists in the work camps scattered around the landscape.[5] They are the FIFO (fly-in fly-out) workers who occupy a "no town" reality,[6] taking shifts that allow them to live at home, fly to work on-site, live in a camp, and very likely never set foot in Fort McMurray itself. In 2012, 28 percent of workers were FIFOs.[7] Air travel is the other modern pipeline carrying workers to and from the oil sands, avoiding the Highway 63's traffic snarls.

The city itself, part of the much larger Regional Municipality of Wood Buffalo (RMWB), sits atop a landscape riddled with speculative extraction leases; speculative not so much because they will warrant a mine or *in situ* extraction process, rather because small players might be bought out by big ones at a profit. Fort McMurray is remote, marooned as if set down by aliens overnight or when the inhabitants of the nearly uninhabited landscape were not watching. So too are the mines and refineries.

Here is Canadian Natural Resources Limited's (CNRL) on-site refinery, which upgrades oil for transport but doesn't make it consumable for commercial markets. It was described

as the biggest industrial project on earth while being built in 2007. Big by what measure is unclear. As a worksite for 14,000 contract workers at any one time? As a materialization of a portion of the $116 billion ($CDN) invested in the oil sands between 2000 and 2010?[8] Certainly not by volume: it produces about 10 percent (140,000 of 1,303,000 barrels per day) of the oil drawn from the open mines of the oil sands.[9] What is big about it is that connectivities from around the world find a node at CNRL. It is the workplace for recent

Heavy haulers at a "big five" producer. At this particular producer site, the soil is very clay-like and it interferes with production on rainy days. During a summer rainstorm, these haulers are grounded because the tires can become full of clay and the trucks begin to swerve off the road when they cannot get a grip (2009). Source: Anonymous, used with permission

migrants from the Middle East employed in on-site worker camp kitchens and, in exception to many of the mines, for temporary foreign workers (usually Chinese) doing welding or other manual labor.

I suggest that Fort McMurray is in an *in-between* moment and is trying to carve something out of that gap. This metaphor has strong resonance in a post-structural understanding of societies where no fixed boundaries may exist, which separate collective and individual identities in "essential" or "natural" ways.[10]

Thus it is possible to make the claim that Fort McMurray is at the crossroads of many things and many people. Passing through it is South Korean-made, industrial-scale equipment, transported to Imperial Oil's Kearl Lake site by way of Washington, Idaho, and Montana; the equipment was too large to be driven through the Rocky Mountains. It is where live-in caregivers, usually from the Philippines, enable Albertan or newly migrated families from eastern Canada to get relatively affordable childcare. It is home to professional, skilled immigrants, recruited directly from the Middle East, India, South America, South Africa, and Australia to meet the technical labor gap and to manage mines. It is a place of speculative capital, of Israeli companies and Chinese foreign interests. It is an incomplete tapestry of people who lack connection to place.

This in-betweenness is in tension with the definitively Fordist nature of some aspects of social life. The "big five" (Suncor, Syncrude, Shell, CNRL, and most recently Imperial) keep wages and benefits competitive. Work, sometimes unionized, is always monotonous and predictable for the heavy-equipment operator and other skilled workers employed directly by the producer. However, as detailed above, other site workers are on contract. Some of them live locally, others commute, others take only the occasional contract, and others quit and are rehired, jumping from one site to another. The "no fixed boundary" exists within a containing relationship (such as an employment relationship), which itself is possibly fluid again (i.e., limited contract). In and out, punctuating permanence and transition, fixity and paternalism, via the producer companies, materialized through the never-ending branding of infrastructure and events. The oil producing companies want to engender a perception of permanence — to overcome the labor shortages — because it keeps everything in flux, just like resource towns always have been.

Current narratives attempt to fix the social and to undermine the waxing and waning of the population that echoes the boom-bust nature of relying on a natural resource. Since 2009, the RMWB has undertaken a rebranding exercise, "Envision Wood Buffalo," which replaces an earlier envisioning project, "Future Forward." In 2011, public charettes asked what, if anything, should Fort McMurray be renamed in attempt to reel in its runaway reputation (of prostitution, drug use, alcoholism, divorce, gambling, crime, and high cost of living… all of which are present, none of which are the definitive identity of Fort McMurray). The municipality produces a biannual magazine, *Big Spirit*; the local community college has hosted the Community Image Summit annually since 2011; a Municipal Development

Plan rewrite in 2011 drew upon public input offered through open houses, charettes, and the "Big Idea" website. A press release announcing the opening of the public input phase of the Municipal Development Plan declared:

> Once again, there is a feeling in the air that our region is on the cusp of something BIG. Traffic is picking up, oil is in demand and media interest in our region is on the rise. The world is catching on to something many people here already know: BIG things are in store for the Wood Buffalo region.[11]

Leadership Wood Buffalo attempts to link residents-as-stakeholders, usually well-educated professionals, with non-profit groups through research projects and, hopefully, eventually by filling positions on their boards of directors. A more recent leadership initiative, Leadership Boot Camp, is pitched at everyone: college and high school-age youth, would-be community leaders, all other stakeholders who want to become "leaders who are optimistic, proactive, big picture, systems thinkers."[12] Social Prosperity Wood Buffalo, a partnership between the RMWB, the Suncor Energy Foundation, and the University of Waterloo, is tasked with enabling capacity-building, fostering networks, and encouraging innovation. Ironically, my research interviews with non-profits in Fort McMurray prior to these last two initiatives, suggest such networking was already happening very organically, if not as comprehensively as a consultant can enable.

So what's the big deal? Or, as that aforementioned press release asks, "How could Wood Buffalo be leading the world?" Go big or go home. Or rather, come home and stay a while. Texas has big ten-gallon hats. Fort McMurray has something big too… something to be determined.

There is very much a mood of "opportunity" — the average annual household income is reportedly $177,000[13] — and "community" among residents, even if they have moved away. People will talk about it being a "family friendly" environment, a direct challenge to the drive-by journalism that paints the town as a victim of Gillette Syndrome (named after Gillette, Wyoming, it encapsulates the social evils that are associated with boomtowns, such as those listed above). There is an assumption of "sameness," for instance, given that every household pays more for housing here than they would anywhere else; up to as much as 70 percent of income. The average house price, in early 2012, was a substantial $751,000. But those houses themselves are the same: a recently built subdivision, Eagle Ridge, is very nearly identical to Edmonton's MacEwan Village (owing to their common developer), however the latter are half the price.

"Sameness" is a movement westward and into a suburb that is neither lowbrow nor banal, nor exclusive and separate; rather, suburban life is the default outcome because there is nothing else available,[14] given that the town was home to only 1,200 in the mid-1960s and the housing stock has grown in boom-bust fits and starts since then.

Municipal involvement in its suburbanization is a process of spatial recategorization and reterritorialization but is always incomplete. Legislatively, the push for land release must come through the province and requires careful negotiation given that the leases overlap geographically into the city itself.

Instead, the municipality is attempting to fix a pleasant, sustainable social reality, a consistent labor force, and adequate social services onto the inevitable flux of a boomtown, the exceptionality of the mines and their ever-shifting roster of workers, the lack of infrastructure, not only roads, but also retail outlets, crowed schools, and an overextended emergency room staff at the local hospital. The in-betweenness is a tension of fixity and mobility, of the flux of daily life in sometimes normal, other times exceptional circumstances. Indeed, residents talk about how Fort McMurray isn't that different from anywhere else, and in many ways it is not. There are swimming lessons, school plays, traffic jams, Canada Day parades, and a layer of big spirit, put forth by the municipality. But there are also exceptions, like relationships ending as abruptly as Highway 63's transformation into a winter-only road north of Fort McMurray, like students who cannot hand in their homework because they've loaned a binder to a friend whose family suddenly moved back to Newfoundland. Also exceptional are the oil companies, which are not necessarily as paternalistic as in earlier resource towns, but which are omnipresent through branded relationships with local institutions. Part of the largest recreational facility in town, and indeed the north, is MacDonald Island Park, home to the Suncor Community Leisure Centre, soon to feature an addition called Shell Place; Keyano College is home to the Syncrude Sport & Wellness Centre; Holy Trinity High School boasts the Suncor Energy Centre for the performing arts; a recent project to evaluate the health needs of the homeless was financed through a $1.2-million legacy gift — upon the departure of the General Manager of Shell Albian Sands — to the Northern Lights Health Foundation[15]; the homeless drop-in center now has an on-site health clinic, "funded through the Northern Lights Health Foundation, Shell Canada, Chevron Canada Ltd., and Marathon Oil Corporation."[16] Big projects, big possibilities through the aggrandizement (biggification?) of everything from the trucks to the price of houses, to the opportunities, to helping the homeless, a group long part of the boomtown's social landscape.[17]

Fort McMurray is a place where the core and periphery, near and far, and contradictory crossroads of are mutually coexistent, not unlike the boundary-space and its boundary objects.[18] That is, it is a place wanting to fix an identity, but full of slippery objects, people, things. It is exceptional — where the periphery meets the core in a folding overlap that challenges the binary nature of these descriptors, a boundary topology[19] — while normal. To fix the social is to place, at the terminus of Highway 63 — the road to riches — a suburban life full of big oil branding and rife with normalized disorder. A place where you're as likely to suddenly move away from your house as you are to spend difficult shifts rumbling along in a truck as big as one.

Endnotes

1 Beyond it lies only Fort McKay, a hamlet of about 500 people who are mostly Metis and First Nations peoples. Thus, Fort McMurray is not literally the end of the highway, but is the place most often associated with the oil sands.

2 Gerson, J. "Alberta's Highway 63, an Oil sands Lifeline, Has Seen 46 Deaths in Five Years." In: *The National Post.* 2012. http://news.nationalpost.com/2012/04/30/albertas-highway-63-an-oil-sands-lifeline-has-seen-46-deaths-in-five-years/, 13.03.13.

3 Ekers, M./Hamel, P./Keil, R. "Governing Suburbia: Modalities and Mechanisms of Suburban Governance." In: *Regional Studies.* 46(3). 2012. p. 412.

4 Images, courtesy of an unnamed source in Fort McMurray, AB, are used with permission.

5 Regional Municipality of Wood Buffalo, Planning and Development Department. *Municipal Census 2012 - Count Yourself In.* 2012.

6 Storey, K. "Fly-in/Fly-out: Implications for Community Sustainability." In: *Sustainability 2.* 2010. p. 1161–1181.

7 Regional Municipality of Wood Buffalo, Planning and Development Department. p. 127.

8 Government of Alberta. *Alberta's Oil Sands, Economic Benefits.* http://www.oilsands.alberta.ca/economicinvestment.html, 14.03.13.

9 Oil Sands Developers Group. *Oil Sands Projects List, March 2013.* http://www.oilsandsdevelopers.ca/wp-content/uploads/2013/03/Oil-Sands-Project-List-March-5-2013.pdf, 12.03.13.

10 Keil, R./Young D. "Introduction: In-Between Canada — The Emergence of the New Urban Middle." In: *In-between Infrastructure: Urban Connectivity in an Age of Vulnerability.* Young, D./Burke Wood, P./Keil, R. (eds.): Praxis (e)Press. 2011. p. 3.

11 Press release, Regional Municipality of Wood Buffalo. *What's the BIG IDEA Launch.* 2011.

12 Leadership Boot Camp. http://www.rmwbleaders.com/index.php/welcome/course_community, 21/03/13.

13 Vanderklippe, N. "Fort McMurray: The Heart of the Oil Patch Seeks its Soul." *The Globe and Mail.* 2012. http://m.theglobeandmail.com/report-on-business/industry-news/energy-and-resources/fort-mcmurray-the-heart-of-the-oil-patch-seeks-its-soul/article2212154/?service=mobile, 07.09.12.

14 Nijman, Jan. "The American Suburb as Utopian Constellation." In: *Suburban Constellations.* Jovis. 2013.

15 Christian, C. "Outgoing Shell GM Says Goodbye at Farewell Ceremony." In: *Fort McMurray Today.* 2011. http://www.fortmcmurraytoday.com/2011/03/04/outgoing-shell-gm-says-goodbye-at-farewell-ceremony, 05.03.13.

16 Thompson, J. "Centre of Hope adds Health Clinic." In: *Fort McMurray Today.* 2012. http://www.fortmcmurraytoday.com/2012/12/13/centre-of-hope-adds-health-clinic, 15.12.12.

17 Thank you to Sara Jackson for the language aggrandizement / biggification.

18 Keil, R./Shields, R. "Suburban Boundaries." In: *Suburban Constellations.* Jovis. 2013.

19 Ibid.

WALKING OUT OF TALLINN
Roger Keil

One night, I simply went on and on, walking all the way down to Houston Street, a distance of some seven miles, and found myself in a state of disorienting fatigue, laboring to remain on my feet. That night I took the subway home, and instead of falling asleep immediately, I lay in bed, too tired to release myself from wakefulness, and I rehearsed in

the dark the numerous incidents and sights I had encountered while roaming, sorting each encounter like a child playing with wooden blocks, trying to figure out which belonged where, which responded to which. Each neighborhood of the city appeared to be made of a different substance, each seemed to have a different air pressure, a different psychic weight: the bright lights and shuttered shops, the housing projects and luxury hotels, the fire escapes and city parks. My futile task of sorting went on until the forms began to morph into each other and assume abstract shapes unrelated to the real city.

Teju Cole, *Open City.* New York: Random House, 2011: 6–7.

4

REGIONS

SUBURBANISMS
IN AFRICA?

Alan Mabin

Iconic contemporary African city
development — old and new on
Guinea Conakry Street, Addis
Ababa, Ethiopia (2013)

Source: Alan Mabin

In what ways does Africa have suburbs? What kinds of suburbanism can be identified in Africa? Or are these terms simply impositions from a developed or Northern/Western world? The indirect answer is that anywhere cities are growing quickly, most of their inhabitants, and indeed passers-by, will be in places that are new relative to original sites and centers. The term "suburban" applies minimally both to many recent areas of expansion and to many older areas, simply conceptualized as "between" old centers and new peripheries. Both of course exist in every African city, so minimally again, Africa's cities have "suburbs" and "suburbanisms" associated with them. Some of them may even look like or feel like suburbs on other continents, but the diversity — not to mention recent appearance of so much African city space and population — means that can hardly be the general case.

African cities are not all growing equally fast,[1] but some have ballooned at breakneck speed. By various estimates Lagos grew to more than fifteen times its independence-date (1960) size, within half a century. Moving south to Luanda, one of the fastest expanding cities in the world, where war, foreign investment in oil, and special kinds of politics have produced a fractured urbanism of massive scale inside a generation. On west and east coasts, Dakar, Luanda, Dar-es-Salaam, and Maputo exhibit diverse patterns: but all are rather different cities each time a resident at the periphery of the city traverses space and visits the old centers (not to mention, each time an occasional visitor returns). For Africa's cities have in general been changing very, very quickly and therefore exhibit new urbanisms and new forms.

What predominates today in the view of observers is not the original form of urbanism. It's not colonial, it's not traditional, it's not simple and indeed it can be exceedingly diverse. The long history of African urbanisms[2] shows recent dramatic acceleration, in common with many Asian places but perhaps distinct too. New spaces and forms produced — the spaces of the new and the creation of space by the new — offer much opportunity for new exploration, and demand new conceptualization.

Recent literature indicates that rapid change is especially concentrated in three kinds of places.[3] First in most accounts, city peripheries, where constant movement of urban frontiers is not merely extending the existing, but creating new kinds of mix and spaces for different urbanisms. Second, older areas between original centers and current edges, which reveal very rapid changes of populations, densities of people and buildings, and activities. Third, new centralities, because both peripheral expansion and redevelopments in older areas destabilize former centralities as they remake patterns of urban life and movement.

Movement of people appears to be ebbing and flowing all the time between multiple spaces, between country and city; and cities internally reveal ebb and flow as they continue to grow. This complexity of movement is illustrated at the peripheries of cities. Some residents find themselves incorporated there as cities expand horizontally and their villages or customary settlements become part of a continuous fabric. Some arrive there from parts of the countryside and seek places to stay around the weakly defined urban edges.[4] But many coming from the countryside seek urban insertion not at the periphery but within the older quarters (as in Kariakoo in Dar es Salaam, central informal settlements like Nairobi's Kibera, or inner-city Johannesburg). At the same time the periphery is a site of opportunity for longer-term urban residents: in a new "planned slum," Ndogbassi, built on the outskirts of Douala in the mid-1970s, Elate explains how residents from the city of Douala, not the rural areas, relocated to Ndogbassi to gain house ownership; and that is one of many cases.[5]

Spaces inside cities also offer various opportunities where newer arrivals of many origins compete and collaborate with those longer established, producing a growing number of centralities. Some are older. Some are very new. Within this flux, words including suburb, periurban, *subúrbio*, township, informal settlement, camp, and others in many more languages than English jostle for meaning.

As Richard Harris asks in his recent review of suburbs at the global scale, is "suburb" or "suburbanism" the best term to capture the process and dynamics that jostle in African cities?[6] Such terms translate poorly from one situation to another, from one city to another, and indeed from one language to another. Starting from English, it is provocative to observe uses of terms close to suburb or given sometimes as equivalents in other languages. English approaches the suburb from the center: but there are other linguistic trajectories. Areas for which "suburb'" is used in English are often approached in African expression from outside the city rather than within. So the parts that come before the city replace the English implications embedded in suburb of moving away from the harder core city and indeed, towards the countryside. In isiZulu one might hear about the *iphethelo ledolobha* (borders and outskirts of the city) also used in general to denote the suburbs, although it is also common in some places for Zulu speakers to talk of *lisabhebe*, obviously derived from the English word.

In colonial languages other than English, such as French and Portuguese, one has to tangle with webs of meaning associated with terms such as *cité* vs. *ville; banlieue* or *faubourg* among others.[7] The Portuguese word *subúrbio* has diverse histories and uses on at least three continents; it has had implications of periphery, the non-urban, a hierarchy of social division of space. According to da Silva Pereira,[8] in Brazilian usage (sometimes influential in shaping language in Angola and Mozambique), subúrbio has come to be "an imprecise expression used everywhere to indicate the *bairros* (quarters) which do not appear on maps and are usually forgotten by public authorities" (my translation). During the colonial period, the word subúrbios emerges in reference not to the white, planned, cement city, but the informal areas of African residence on the periphery, where land was rented from elite settler landholders[9] as well as allocated through chiefly systems.

For Morais and Raposo and Oppenheimer and Raposo,[10] the "model of the colonial town … persists'" in some of the older spaces, while simultaneously another model of the urban is conceived "at its margins," where material conditions can be precarious and spatial organization has not followed any specific urban plan.

Densification around Shekilango
Road, Dar es Salaam, Tanzania
(2008)
Source: Alan Mabin

Ubongo area, Dar es Salaam,
Tanzania (2008)
Source: Alan Mabin

Maputo, Moçambique: Bairro
Laulane planned area of 1980s
(2008)

Source: Jorgen Anderson
www.homespace.dk

Soweto suburbanizing, Johannesburg, South Africa (2006)
Source: Alan Mabin

Suburbs and peripheries take as many or even more forms in various African contexts as they do elsewhere. Older versions include townships and *bidonvilles*, housing estates for colonial officials, as well as all kinds of self-built city zones. They include spaces that concentrate new economic activities, zones of middle- and upper-income residence, some of them gated; they reveal diverse meanings of informality of building, land markets and social activity. Suburban growth has many drivers, shaped by policy and institutional mechanisms, which try to direct urban growth, and by the reality of what happens in practice, which often reveals very little impact of planning at all. The key actors involved in African suburban growth are of course, also diverse — property developers, landowners, traditional authorities, administrators, households, associations, politicians, with perhaps a larger influence in many cases from far away (in the past European colonial offices, nowadays China and India for example), than is associated with local suburban development in some other parts of the world.

In all their complexity, African city spaces and styles, whatever words we use, contribute an expanding part of global suburbanisms. For the present and to generalize, the word suburb can be retained for many peripheral and not-so-peripheral areas — indeed sometimes not far from being central — in many African cities. What is interesting about these quarters is that they are changing, sometimes very quickly. For example, there are low-density residential zones that are fast becoming high density, such as eight-story buildings replacing simple Swahili houses in Dar es Salaam, or office buildings supplanting bungalows in Durban. What types of work can advance thinking about African suburbs and what research themes appear possible and valuable?

-The moving edge is where much of the literature is focused: analyses of ways in which informality, conflict, and power intersect speak powerfully to ways in which the rest of the world is increasingly working;
-Change in older suburbs is less closely observed but enormously significant;
-New centralities or perhaps better, new stages for urban life are appearing, and only beginning to enter the pages of academic representation.
In what ways do Africa's (new) suburbs/suburbanisms suggest new urbanisms and ideas of urbanisms, to others?

The term suburban has frequently been negatively applied. It can mean "less than" rather than "not fully" urban. Statements like this would potentially denigrate most space in Africa's cities as not-yet, not-fully, or not-adequately urban. Scholarly authors addressing suburbanisms in Africa avoid creating a morality of urbanisms and suburbanisms; there is a sense of searching for "the city yet to come."[11] Moreover, the suburb has also come to mean something about the *new* in acts of claiming the periphery. The probability is that peripheral spaces and quarters are those of the most creative in music, art, and new forms of expression and of being.[12] And the energy of the newer, even outer areas may be an important sign of changes in spatialities of creativity and the "now" not only in African places but in Paris and other northern metropolises where today, it can be the banlieue which provides the *it* factor — *qui donne le là!*

There are camps, townships, suburbs and sub-urbanisms in Africa. Varied forms of suburbanism combine to provide distinctively new terrain for urban life in Africa.[13] The search for languages and understandings will continue and grow as the cities themselves become the second continent of urbanism and indeed suburbanisms, after Asia in scale, in the coming decades.

Endnotes

1   Potts, D. *Circular Migration in Zimbabwe and Contemporary Sub-Saharan Africa.* London: James Currey. 2010.
2   Freund, Bill. *The African City: A History.* Cambridge: Cambridge University Press. 2007.
3   Mabin, A./Butcher, S./ Bloch, R. "Peripheries, Suburbanisms and Change in Sub-Saharan African Cities." In: *Social Dynamics.* Forthcoming.
4   As discussed by: Harris, R. "Meaningful Types in a World of Suburbs." In: *Research in Urban Sociology.* 10. 2010. p. 15–47.
5   Elate S.S. "African Urban History in the Future." In: Falola T./Salm, S.J. (eds.): *Globalization and Urbanization in Africa.* Trenton, NJ and Asmara, Eritrea: Africa World Press. 2004. p. 51–66.
6   Ibid., p. 25.
7   Topalov, C./ Coudroy de Lille, L./ Depaule, J.C./ Marin, B.(eds.): *L'Aventure des Mots de la Ville: à Travers le Temps, les Langues, les Sociétés.* Paris: Robert Laffont. 2010.
8   da Silva, P. "Suburbio." In: Topalov et al., (eds.): *L'Aventure des Mots de la Ville: à Travers le Temps, les Langues, les Sociétés.* Paris: Robert Laffont. 2010. p. 1203

9   Jenkins, P. "African Cities: Competing Claims on Urban Land." In:Locatelli, F./ Nugent, P. (eds.): *African Cities: Competing Claims Over Urban Spaces.* Leiden: Brill. 2009. p. 81–108.
10 Morais, J./Raposo, I. "Da Cidade Colonial às Novas Urbes Africanas: Notas Exploratórias." In: *Cidades Africanas, Cadernos da Faculdade de Arquitectura da Universidade Técnica de Lisboa.* Lisboa. Universidade Técnica de Lisboa, 2005. p. 88–91; Oppenheimer, J./ Raposo, I.,(eds.). *Subúrbios de Luanda e Maputo.* Lisboa: Edições Colibri. 2007; Luanda and *musseques* are also cited in this regard in; Roque, S. Ambitions of Cidade: *War-Displacement and Concepts of the Urban among Bairro Residents in Benguela, Angola.* Unpublished doctoral dissertation. University of Cape Town. 2009.
11 Simone, A.M. *For the City Yet to Come: Changing African Life in Four Cities.* Durham: Duke University Press. 2004.
12 da Silva, 2010. Op. cit. p. 1204.
13 Bloch, R. *Africa's New Suburbs: Growth, Expansion and Governance.* Draft Paper for the Global Suburbanisms Workshop on Suburban Governance, Leipzig, July 1–2, 2011.

THE AMERICAN SUBURB AS UTOPIAN CONSTELLATION

Jan Nijman

Townhouse development in an
inner suburb of Toronto (2007)
Source: Stephen Mak

North America may well be considered the birthplace of the prototypical twentieth-century suburb. In the wake of the Second World War, the process of suburbanization accelerated to such unprecedented levels that it fundamentally reordered the US city. Common usage of the terms "suburb" and "suburbanization" spread to the rest of the western world, and then across the globe.

The traditional American notion of the suburb connotes a settled, stable, situation. Certainly this applied to the 1950s idea of the suburb where white middle classes families had "arrived." The suburb embodied the achievement of an ideal, the good life; it was harmonious, predictable, and secure, and change was not a part of that dreamy constellation. It appears that, in the United States at least, the imaginary of suburban utopia has proven a great deal more tenacious than its material counterpart.

The origins of suburbanization in North America predate the 1950s by at least 100 years. In preindustrial times, suburbs were viewed as undesirable and shady places on the edge of town; marginal neighborhoods with a mix of the poor and people with licentious habits. The word "urbane" referred to sophistication, elegance, and high-class. The elites occupied the center of these compact preindustrial cities that mixed residential and economic functions (i.e., trade, services).

This arrangement came to an end with the Industrial Revolution. Cities became sites of industrial production, often with detrimental environmental effects, and they grew much more dense. This resulted in a growing interest of the elites in new housing on the urban periphery: home as a refuge from work, as a source of happiness and goodness.[1] Upper-class status became associated with mansions on large estates in a quiet, lush, suburban environment, while the city center turned into a scene of congestion, pollution, crime, and crowded working class residential areas.

The new suburbia of the mid-nineteenth century in places such as West Philadelphia was an expression of class wealth and elitism. It was driven by bourgeois demand for grand suburban living. In Canada, early suburbanization moved somewhat slower and once it gathered momentum, as in the Beach area of Toronto in the latter part of the nineteenth century, it was more a mixture of upper- and middle- class populations. In Toronto and other Canadian cities, suburban densities were (and often are today) higher than in the United States.[2]

Suburbanization proceeded faster in the United States than anywhere else because industrialization was more vigorous and sustained, and as such fueled a more significant reordering of cities. By the late nineteenth century, the US had become the biggest industrial power — and the most suburbanized country — in the world.

And there was another, cultural, reason: the individualized, nuclear, family was very much an American institution (closely related to the "American Dream") and demanded a single family home, which was easier to realize in the spacious suburbs than in the city center. "Unlike any other affluent civilization, Americans have idealized the house and yard rather than the model neighborhood or the ideal town."[3] The almost spiritual journey to (and commercial perversion of) suburban utopia was at times expressed in religious metaphors: in 1921, the *National Real Estate Journal* wrote that the "Garden of Eden" was the "first subdivision." The new suburb was at once frontier and destiny.

On the ground, suburban realities were changing. From the latter part of the nineteenth century until the Second World War, suburbanization was increasingly accompanied by the relocation of economic activity and jobs away from the central city, with decentralized manufacturing areas emerging everywhere from Los Angeles to Toronto to Boston.[4] The introduction of the electric streetcar in the 1890s pushed suburbanization along and, increasingly, the middle and lower middle classes were following the elite out of the central city.[5] West Philadelphia was one of the biggest suburbs of that era, doubling in population to 200,000 between 1890 and 1910.

The rhetoric of suburban utopia became increasingly incongruous with the evolving metropolitan realities. One aspect of this is that the suburbanization of the working classes and of ethnic minorities was often crowded out of the prevailing market-generated narratives of continued exclusivity and privilege. We should not underestimate how much these narratives have shaped academic writings on the subject: Wiese observes, wryly, that "historians have done a better job excluding African Americans from the suburbs than even white suburbanites."[6]

Calgary suburbs in March
(2013)
Source: Roger Keil

The land development and real estate industry began to target potential first-time homebuyers. "Why Pay Rent" campaigns from around the turn of the century promoted suburban living to middle- and working-class households. Not unlike the fate met by home buyers in the early twenty-first century (!), many were lured into homeownership they could barely afford, struggling "up a down escalator" entranced with dreams of economic security, saddled with debt, and confused by a false sense of social mobility.[7]

Increasingly, demand for suburban living was stimulated and fabricated on the supply side. From the turn of the century, developers began to promote urban peripheries, often working in partnership with transit owners, utility companies, and local government. It had become increasingly difficult to separate the suburban dreams of American families from the marketing endeavors of the building industry. And there was much more to come.

From 1950 to 1980, the suburban population of the United States tripled; by 1970, more people lived in suburbs than in either central cities or in the countryside. The United States had become a "suburban nation."[8]

The canalized suburbs of Fort
Lauderdale, Florida (2012)
Source: Sameer Gupta

Demand for housing after the war was significantly up and corporate interests and government regulations converged like never before to promote single housing home ownership in the suburbs. Homeownership and automobile ownership escalated in tandem. The construction of Levittown, the archetypal 1950s suburb, was the well-documented result of these new governance modalities.

Suburbanization was the business of an extremely powerful industrial conglomerate that employed (and helped generate) the American suburban imaginary to full effect. It included huge corporations such as General Motors (which offered a helping hand in the demise of the electric streetcar) and General Electric (which had embarked on the mass production of household appliances for single-family homes); local "growth machines" consisting of developers, builders, and banks; local governments that provided conducive zoning and building regulatory frameworks, and sometimes direct subsidies; and, last but not least, a federal government that was central to the financing of homeownership, the construction of highways, and that in various ways espoused suburban ideologies.

This convergence of market and government in the pursuit of suburbanization, unchecked as it often seemed in the United States, was less extreme in Canada.[9] It is no coincidence that the North American city best known for its efforts to control suburbanization lies in Canada. "Vancouverism" refers to that's city's self-declared defiance of suburbanization pressures and its stand for "responsible" urban planning. [10]

Across the United States, suburban utopia was readied for mass-commodification; it became part and parcel of the American Dream:

> There are two mythic journeys in the US. The first … was the trek to the West, ending in California. The second, the archetypal journey of the mid-twentieth century, was from the city to the suburbs. … it was a quest signifying acculturation, Americanization, and ultimately success. In this second mythic American journey, the family car replaced the covered wagon, and the single-family home displaced the family homestead as iconic representations. [11]

Since the early 1960s, the suburban ideal was conveniently (if inadvertently) sustained by the decline of central cities across the continent as a result of deindustrialization and selective outmigration. The suburb was everything the city was not: clean, green, spacious, safe, quiet, harmonious, predictable, and homogeneous.

Various kinds of economic activity and work have also suburbanized in a variety of patterns of "edge cities"[12] and "edgeless cities."[13] By the mid-nineties, about twice as many people commuted to work within suburbs as commuted between them and cities.[14] Presently, nearly half of the US metropolitan population works in locations more than ten miles from downtown and only about one-fifth has a workplace within three miles of downtown.[15]

Soon, architectural critics began to depict suburbs as lowbrow, boring, and banal. The

monotonous, mass-produced, subdivisions of the postwar years certainly were a long way from the carefully designed elite suburban mansions of the early nineteenth century. More importantly, suburban culture as a whole came to be regarded as uninteresting, conservative, and spiritless. It was not hard to discern elitist undertones in such critiques. Examples include: "Jane Jacobs's (1961) picture of her own idyllically bohemian Lower Manhattan neighborhood in *The Death and Life of Great American Cities*[16], and the wild anger at suburban piggery that pervades James Howard Kunstler's (1993) *The Geography of Nowhere*."[17] The aesthetic devaluation of suburbs coincided with increased access to suburbs by lower-income strata of the population, even if a home in the suburbs was still sold as a privileged place in the sun along with all the traditional narratives of the past.[18] Suburban poverty increased and suburbs were increasingly subject to fiscal stress, crime, and social problems like housing deterioration, homelessness, or drug abuse. By 2010, more people lived in poverty in the suburbs than did in central cities. Between 2000 and 2008, suburbs in the country's largest metro areas saw their poor population grow by 25 percent — almost five times faster than primary cities. At the same time, suburbs were catching up with central cities in terms of ethnic diversity: the 2010 US Census reported that well over a third of the suburban population is now "non-white." The proportion of foreign immigrants has also been increasing faster in suburbs than in central cities, both in the US and in Canada. The suburban population has continued to grow apace, but increasingly it isn't because

Barrie, Ontario suburb (2012)
Source: Roger Keil

Americans are passionately pursuing their dreams and seeing them fulfilled; it is because many people don't have anywhere else to go. If homeownership is the goal, there is little else than the suburbs, and at an ever-greater distance from the city. Increasingly, then, suburban living for many people has become less a matter of choice and more a matter of financial constraints and necessity.

This does not mean that individual suburbs are no longer exclusive. Quite to the contrary, since the 1960s, we have witnessed the emergence of a kaleidoscope of suburbs that are highly distinct and often segregated on the basis of socioeconomic status and ethnicity, precisely because suburbanization has become so massive. Suburbanization has fueled metropolitan fragmentation in terms of governance structures, particularly in the United States. There are in the United States presently about 90,000 local governments including municipalities, towns, townships, school districts, water management districts, and so on; these are all local government institutions. The combined number of municipalities and town(ships) is about 19,500, compared to 16,800 in 1952. The difference points to roughly 2,700 incorporations in the past half-century, most driven by consideration of fiscal independence and/or spatial exclusion.

Vaughan, Ontario suburb (2011)
Source: Roger Keil

At the sub-local residential level, the trends are astonishing: between 1970 and 2011, the number of association-governed residential communities rose from 10,000 to 314,200. Today, more than 62 million people in the United States reside in association-governed communities: homeowners associations, condominiums, cooperatives and other planned communities.[19]

The patterns of local and sub-local government and governance vary considerably across the United States, and it's all about scale. The gradual growth and expansion of older American cities has generally resulted in a steady increase of the number of local governments (municipalities, school districts, and other taxing authorities).

The Chicago metropolitan area, for example, contains no fewer than 569 local governments. At the other extreme, the Las Vegas metro area has only thirteen local governments. This does not mean, however, that Las Vegas is less fragmented and more centrally governed, in fact the opposite is true. The difference lies in the relative importance of private sub-local governance. In more recent metropolitan areas like Las Vegas, private sub-local governance is much more prevalent than in Chicago and their territories tend to be smaller than the typical municipal suburb of Chicago.[20] The most salient design that has accompanied the rise of private governance is, of course, the gated community.

America's suburban landscape today is more varied than ever and filled with contradictions. Suburbs range in character from Virginia's massive Tyson's Corner to America's "first suburban Chinatown" in Monterey Park, to the traditional upscale neighborhoods of Montreal West. Some are, as in the early days, extraordinarily wealthy and privileged, others are very poor; some are class-based, others are ethnic enclaves; some are entirely residential, others are mixed-use; some have evolved for over a century, others emerged in the past decade; some are a residence of first choice, others a suburb of last resort. And most tend to be homogeneous or exclusive one way or the other. Single metropolitan areas the size of, say, the San Francisco Bay Area, have become enormous multi-nodal puzzles that even local residents have the hardest time figuring out.[21]

This short history of the North American suburb would not be complete without mentioning one last development that, in a way, makes it come full circle. The blurring between city and suburb has been reinforced in recent years by a "return" to the city of middle- and upper-middle class households. Many city centers have witnessed the gentrification of once-derelict neighborhoods, especially in the United States.[22]

From New York's Harlem to downtown Miami, wealth is coming back into the city and there is a growing number of gentry households who want it all: comfortable roomy living, a parking space, a lively hip neighborhood, a range of urban amenities in walking distance, as well as a good school for the kids. For those who can afford it, there's a suburban utopia in the center of the city.

Endnotes

1 Fishman, R. "Bourgeois Utopias: Visions of Suburbia." Reprinted in: Fainstein, S./Campbell, S. (eds.): *Readings in Urban Theory*. Oxford: Blackwell. 2002 [1987]. p. 21–31.

2 Harris, R./Lewis, R. "The Geography of North American Cities and Suburbs, 1900-1950." In: *Journal of Urban History*. 27(3). 2001. p. 262–292.

3 Hayden, D. *Building Suburbia: Green Fields and Urban Growth, 1820–2000*. New York: Pantheon Books. 2003. p. 5–6.

4 Walker, R./ Lewis, R.D. "Beyond the Crabgrass Frontier: Industry and the Spread of North American Cities, 1850-1950." In: *Journal of Historical Geography*. 27(1). 2001. p. 3–19.

5 Warner, S.B. Jr. *Streetcar Suburbs: The Process of Growth in Boston, 1870-1900*. Cambridge: Harvard University Press. 1962.

6 Wiese, A. "Places of our Own. Suburban Black Towns Before 1960." In: *Journal of Urban History*. 19(3). 1993. p. 30–54.

7 Edel, M./Sclar, E.D./Luria, D. *Shaky Palaces: Homeownership and Social Mobility in Boston's Suburbanization*. New York: Columbia University Press. 1984.

8 Muller, P. O. *Contemporary Suburban America*. New Jersey. Englewood Cliffs. 1981.
Duany, A./Plater-Zyberk, E./Speck, J. *Suburban Nation: The Rise of Sprawl and the Decline of the American Dream*. New York: North Point Press. 2001.

9 Hamel, P./Keil, R. (eds) *Global Suburbanisms*. University of Toronto Press. 2013.

10 Siemiatycki, E./Peck, J,/Wyly, E. Vancouver's Suburban Involution. Forthcoming.

11 Hanlon, B./Short, J.R./Vicino, T.J. *Cities and Suburbs: New Metropolitan Realities in the United States*. Oxford. Routledge. 2010. p. 6.

12 Garreau, J. *Edge City: Life on the New Frontier*. New York: Doubleday. 1991.

13 Lang, R. E.. *Edgeless Cities*. Washington, DC: Brookings Institution Press. 1993.

14 Sharpe, W./ Wallock, L.. "Bold New City or Built-Up 'Burb? Redefining Contemporary Suburbia." In: *American Quarterly*. 46(1). 1994. p. 1–30.

15 Brookings Institution. *The State of Metropolitan America: Suburbs and the 2010 Census*. Washington DC. 2011.

16 Jacobs, J. *The Death and Life of Great American Cities*. New York: The Modern Library. 1961.

17 Kunstler, J. H. *The Geography of Nowhere: The Rise and Decline of America's Man-Made Landscape*. New York: Touchstone. 1993.
Seal, C. "We Built this Suburb." In: *The Yale Review of Books*. New Haven. 2003. 10.04.12. http://www.yalereviewofbooks.com/archive/spring04/review01.shtml.htm.

18 Knox, P. L. *Metroburbia, USA*. New Brunswick: Rutgers University Press. 2008.

19 Community Associations Institute, Falls Church, VA. Industry Data. 2012. www.caionline.org/info/research/Pages/default.aspx. 10.02.13.

20 Nelson, R. H. The Rise of Sublocal Governance. *Working Paper #09–45*, Mercatus Center, George; Mason University, Washington, DC. 2009.

21 Walker, R./Schafran, A. The Strange Case of the Bay Area. Forthcoming.

22 Sharpe/Wallock, 1994. Op. cit.

LATIN AMERICA AT THE URBAN MARGIN: SOCIO-SPATIAL FRAGMENTATION AND AUTHORITARIAN GOVERNANCE

Dirk Heinrichs & Henning Nuissl

Favela, Rio de Janeiro,
January (2005)
Source: Roger Keil

Latin America is one of the most urbanized regions worldwide and location of some of the largest urban agglomerations. From their origins as colonial settlements, these cities have seen dramatic functional, economic and social transformations, and suburbanization has been one of the most prominent attributes of this change.

The origins of what can be termed suburbanization date from the beginning of the twentieth century, when the urban elites started to abandon their homes in the center of the cities and moved towards out-of-town settlements. In the following decades, primarily the larger cities witnessed a dramatic increase in population in consequence of rural-urban migration of peasants from the countryside. The population of Mexico City grew from about 2.5 million in 1950 to almost 11 million in 1975, while the city of São Paulo saw a rise from 2.3 to 10 million over the same period. With national and local governments unable to cope with this massive rural-urban migration, cities saw the development of informal self-built settlements on vacant land at the urban fringe. They were characterized by makeshift buildings, narrow access roads, high levels of crowding and the absence of service facilities like water and electricity. Over the subsequent decades a share of these settlements have undergone significant consolidation in terms of building structure, services as well as social structure and organization. Others have turned into areas of physical and social despair.

Since the 1970s, state-led public and social housing construction has made and continues to make a significant contribution to suburbanization in many cities in the region. In many countries, national governments initiated programs for low-income housing to reduce housing deficits as well as to replace informal buildings. In Chile for example, the Ministry of Housing and Urban Development (MINVU) created a basic housing program in 1980. Between 1990 and 2005, about 2.3 million houses were built with some form of government support, which means that about 25 percent of the country's houses received some form of support from the program.[1] As land prices play a major role in the cost of housing construction, these housing programs likewise find a location in the urban periphery where land is comparatively cheap.

A new form of residential suburbanization is now emerging. Large-scale residential complexes are spreading on the outskirts of cities, often in combination with shopping malls, industrial and exurban office parks, which are at best loosely connected to the existing urban fabric.[2] These mega-projects usually comprise their own urban infrastructure including, for example, retail outlets, recreational amenities and educational facilities. Most of these developments are separated from the public by a gate, fence, or wall and are equipped with enhanced security devices. In addition, they often go hand in hand with the construction of new access and supply infrastructure like highways that connect the new settlements to the central areas of the cities, the main location of jobs and education. The size of such developments varies from a few to tens of thousands of units.

There appears to be a tendency towards a larger scale of development, mainly for two reasons. First, profitability for the developers rises with size. Secondly, larger compounds pro-

The images in this chapter reflect suburban reality in Santiago de Chile: Here, a man moving into his new social housing unit (2008)

An aunt and her niece in their self-built neighborhood (2008)

Source: Andre Künzelmann, Helmholtz Centre for Environmental Research

vide sufficient space to separate new complexes (as walled designs do) from the adjacent lower-class settlements from the former phase of suburbanization.[3]

Corresponding to the traditional trend of the urban elites to escape the squalor of the inner city, some suburban gated communities in Latin America offer large-size, single-family detached houses integrated into the surrounding landscape and are only affordable for upper-income groups. In this form, they connect to the much earlier form of the country club.[4] However, Latin America's recent mega-projects are by no means restricted to the affluent population, but have likewise reached middle- and lower-income groups. For example, a few mega-projects have been developed in Santiago de Chile, which are primarily designed to serve the housing demands of middle-class households. Another example is the Ciudad Verde (Green City) at the periphery of the fast-growing city of Bogotá. This development is currently being built primarily as a social housing project for at least 36,000 households on an area of about 330 hectares of previously agricultural land. This project will include a hospital, a library, two schools, and recreational areas. Gigantic developments for low-priced housing have also emerged on the fringes of Mexico City and Guadalajara but these are privately financed. The layout and architecture of these areas is of course much less elaborated than in the case of the more distinguished projects.

As a consequence of these parallel developments, the clear segregation between socioeconomic strata that has long been a key feature of cities in Latin America has started to change in recent decades. The current wave of suburbanization leads to a sociospatial fragmentation at a much smaller territorial scale and with contrary results. On the one hand, the arrival of residential communities for middle- and upper-class households in traditionally poor municipalities leads to a closer proximity between distinct social groups, because in contrast to other parts in the world, this trend is not associated with the expulsion or replacement of the poorer residents.

On the other hand, segregation scales are still growing in some peripheral areas with predominantly low-income families because of ongoing construction of new budget housing complexes either by private investors or within the framework of welfare housing schemes. In most of the latter areas, quality of life is generally very low, with the need for extremely long commuting trips being a particular drawback for residents.

The case of suburban mega-projects highlights how the physical appearance of contemporary suburbia and its consequences for social and spatial organization are not the only differences from traditional suburban settings in Latin America. Also, the mode by which present-day suburbia is produced is significantly changing. The self-led informal periurban growth of the mid-twentieth century has given way to contemporary suburban development, which one could define as a new authoritarian mode of governance.

This new modality of suburban governance rests on a couple more fundamental trends. On the one hand, the dominating policy of import substitution of the mid-twentieth century was followed by a strong trend towards structural adjustment policies and a generally neoliberal development paradigm in almost all Latin American countries over roughly the last quarter of the century. This went hand in hand with a tendency of governments and authorities to perceive urban growth as an engine of economic growth and a means to attract international capital to the country. The suburban realm therefore has been discovered as a resource for development and economic growth. International companies have appeared on the Latin American real estate markets alongside established national enterprises, but the latter are also increasingly operating as agents of international investment capital.

Today, suburban governance in Latin America is largely characterized by a "restricted role of the state" and a "governing role of private capital." The state's main concern has become to provide the enabling conditions for economic growth in general and private real estate investments in particular.[5]

The changing roles of the state and the private sector become tangible in a few more specific features and typical outcomes of suburban governance in Latin America:

-In several Latin American cities, strategic planning is doing away with the paradigm of the welfare state — i.e., the idea to deploy rational plans that ideally safeguard the balancing of interests and social equity — and has already led to the relaxation and watering down of existing planning regulations that aim at the preservation of a compact urban form.

-While suburban municipalities are often inclined to engage in the legal preparation for urban expansion because investment realized on their territory is key to raise their revenue, recent decentralization policies in many Latin American countries have transferred more planning powers to local authorities and thereby eased their strategy to legally provide for new development.

-Many recent suburban developments were massively supported by investments in the extension of the transport infrastructure (mainly highways) into the city region, either by direct public investments or by the transfer of construction and operation to the private sector through public-private partnership arrangements.

-Very often, the enabling regulation occurs outside normal land use plans and zoning ordinances and take special forms. The Ciudad Verde project, highlighted above is carried by a national government legislation dedicated to fast-track large-scale social housing development. Elsewhere, like in Santiago, this type of development is made possible through so-called conditional urban planning.

-The enabling attitude of state authorities towards the real estate business is sometimes corroborated by existing personal relationships. In Chile, for example, it is no secret that real estate and building investors traditionally have strong personal links to the country's political elites.

The "restricted role of the state" and the "governing" role of capital, which together largely characterize governance at the urban margins in Latin America, associate with several other manifestations of "authoritarian" urban governance that are widely acknowledged in the academic literature.

One is the proliferation of gated communities that have spread in cities across the region. A second aspect is the emergence of privately built and operated access and supply infrastructure. A third element is the rise of homeowners associations and private managerial firms that displace the local state in the governance of local affairs. These phenomena are clearly present in the current trends of suburbanization in Latin America.

These trends are in line with authoritarian modes of city-making, whichhave been observed elsewhere in the wake of globalization. However, one should be cautious with overgeneralizations that disregard regional and local circumstances. There certainly are peculiarities to the Latin American context that shape urban development trends in specific ways, including: a marked centralism of most states with strong national governments, a pronounced segregation of social classes, and a traditionally strong orientation of Latin Americans towards urban centers.

Overall, the contemporary round of suburbanization in Latin America is by no means the only, inevitable result of the individual households' demand for suburban housing (supported by economic and social factors) but also the product of government policies.

Suburban development and land use are strongly driven by the interests of the real estate industry. The major driving force here is not the authoritarian state (as was the case in many Latin American states in the mid-twentieth century) but the "governing" role of capital.

Endnotes

1 Brain, I., P./Mora, A./Rasse, F./Sabatini., F. Social Housing in Chile. Working Paper. Santiago de Chile: Pontificia Universidad Católica de Chile. 2009.

2 Heinrichs, D./Lukas, M./Nuissl, H. "Privatization of the Fringes– a Latin American Type of Post-Suburbia? The Case of Santiago de Chile." In: *Governing Post-Suburban Growth*. Phelps, N./Wu, F. Basingstoke (eds.): Palgrave. 2011. p. 101–121.

3 Sabatini, F./Salcedo, R. "Understanding Deep Urban Change: Patterns of Residential Segregation in Latin American Cities". In: The City, Revisited: *Urban Theory from Chicago, Los Angeles, and New York*. ed.

Judd, D.R./Simpson, D. Minneapolis: University of Minnesota Press. 2011. p. 332–355.

4 Borsdorf, A./Hidalgo, R. "From Polarization to Fragmentation: Recent changes in Latin American Urbanization." In: *Decentralized Development in Latin America: Experiences in Local Governance and Local Development*, ed. Van Lindert, P./Verkoren, O. Santiago de Chile: Geo-Journal Library 97. 2010. p. 23–34.

5 De Mattos, C.A. "Globalización y Metamorfosis Metropolitana en América Latina. De la Ciudad a lo Urbano Generalizado." In: *Revista de Geografía Norte Grande*. 2010. 47. p. 81–104.

GLOBAL SUBURBANISMS: NAVIGATING BY THE CONSTELLATION OF EUROPE

Nicholas A. Phelps

Suburb, Zurich Nord (July 2010)
Source: Roger Keil

It is certain that the center of gravity in trends regarding contemporary urbanization and indeed suburbanization in the world has shifted decisively in this century to Asia and to China in particular. Nevertheless, and at the risk of inviting the accusation of my wanting a perhaps premature return to Western-centered urban theory, I want to celebrate the centrality of "old" Europe to an understanding of global suburbanisms. The constellation of European suburbs from north to south and from east to west in itself contains a world old and new, fast and slow changing. As I have suggested elsewhere, this is Europe as an exporter and importer — a relay — of many of the elements that make up the suburban matrix globally.[1]

Europe encapsulates some of the world's oldest suburbs. It also is home to perhaps the oldest meaning attached to the term *sub*urb, as settlement literally less than urban. Here the original meaning of the term suburb denoted an area of often marginalized populations and unwanted or noxious land uses that settled outside the walls of ancient and medieval cities. The walls in many instances have disappeared or crumbled, though for some European settings the suburbs remain a location in which particular populations — the poor, immigrants — can be defined and marginalized or excluded from national urban society.

In the most conspicuous of contemporary instances of the suburb as exclusionary space, governments sought cheap suburban land for their social housing complexes. These were vertical cities whose radiance has become tarnished over the years. Tarnished by a selective corralling of populations so effective that they might as well have been walled off from the remainder of the suburbs in which they sat, as with the *banlieu* of suburban Paris, or tarnished by their splendid isolation at some reach from the city proper, as with the likes of Rome's Corviale. So effectively have the historic cores of some cities such as Paris been socially cleansed and "Disneyfied" that real life lies outside, in the suburbs, to the point where a niche tourism industry now runs excursions.[2]

In its original sense, then, the suburb represented an approach to the city, which had since ancient times conferred a sense of entitlement, of citizenship, and of access to everything from the necessaries to the elegancies of life. And for many Mediterranean cities, settlement at the periphery continues to entail a sense of *astyphilia*, a Greek term indicating a fondness for the city.[3] Here, then, the suburbs of Athens, Barcelona, Madrid, Rome, and cities elsewhere in the south of Europe, have been important relays for models of civic and political organization surrounding demands for the rights to the city found perhaps at their strongest in a Latin world beyond, and yet intimately connected to, Europe. Some of Europe's suburbs, old and new, therefore provide us with a timely reminder that a second and altogether different meaning attached to the term suburb, which has come to color virtually all popular and academic understandings of the modern suburb, need not, and ought not, overly color our appreciation of the value and possibility of suburbs.

This second meaning of the suburb as one of bourgeois escape from the city in search of space and an engagement with nature has been depicted as one that is universal.[4] In Europe alone, never mind elsewhere, the suburb as bourgeois escape is perhaps most relevant in the north but far less so in the south.

Alongside Europe's ancient and old suburbs, the suburbs of travel by foot and animal and old suburbs of travel by carriage, stand suburbs and processes of suburbanization in Europe as new as anything to be found in Asia. Office and retail decentralization saw Fordist service suburbs such as greater London's Croydon celebrate a modernity that rapidly has been over-taken by the almost unimaginably flexible and decentered, digital, post-Fordist economy.

Yet, Europe has its own spaces of this post-Fordist economy. They are, in important in-stances, suburban in location. At the edge of Zurich, in Freienbach, office blocks of glo-balized financial institutions have nestled curiously among chalets to project formerly low-density residential suburbs and periurban areas stealthily into economic centers of in-dustries of global proportion and reach.[5] The high-tech industries of Montpellier's science park "technopoles" as with others such as Sofia Antipolis were designed as new suburban science cities. These muscular suburban "flexspaces" compete vigorously on the interna-tional stage with the likes of US "edge cities", new townships in China and the cybercities and science cities of Malaysia, India, Japan, and Taiwan.

In Britain, the suburb as bourgeois retreat from the city carved out and tamed nature in manicured gardens rather like miniature versions of manicured aristocratic estates. More or less as a whole, Britain's cities are of what might be regarded elsewhere in mainland Europe as suburban density and morphology. Terraced houses with their backyards or gardens have only sporadically given way to the density of high-rise apartments. Important British plan-ning models such as Ebenezer Howard's Garden City have remained steadfast in their desire to house population in a nature tamed. More surprising is that this peculiarly British tem-plate has proved so appealing and adaptable in its depiction of a new *sub*urbanity that it has been exported internationally and so vigorously.

In some contrast, in Scandinavian places such as the Tapiola garden suburb near Helsinki and Skjettenbyen near Olso, suburban residential development sought to integrate itself more gradually or even seamlessly with nature, producing at times remarkable and striking modernist suburban housing amidst nature. Yet elsewhere, in the south of Europe, nature has in instances been denuded and degraded in the rush to approach the city. On the outskirts of Athens in Kifissia, the new or abandoned *polykatoikia* (regular block-like hous-ing structures with multiple floors) sit amidst rough patches of idle land, some with their columns sprouting the steel bars that will reinforce another floor to be built at some later, unspecified, date as income and opportunity allow.

Elsewhere in the same municipality, this piecemeal degradation of nature has given way to its deliberate destruction as fires are set as a prelude to lucrative suburban residential devel-opments on the favored cool lower slopes of Mount Pelion.[6]

Undoubtedly, Old Europe has its slow changing suburbs, residential suburbs that have changed incrementally and, in some instances, almost imperceptibly; here a loft conversion, there a conservatory added.[7] However, it also bears the scars of extremely rapid development of the city denied for years by socialist central planning; an excess of demand of all sorts — for shops, factories, warehouses, mass residential accommodation, as well as more exclusive gated residential developments — spilling out, as new suburbs gorge themselves on the expanses of agricultural land now available through often imperfectly reconstructed market mechanisms.

The new suburbs appear not as incremental outward expansion of the city but in massive array on the edges of Leipzig or Budapest; as a rupture with past patterns of socialist and pre-socialist urbanization.[8] Moreover, they appear almost regardless of the fortunes of these cities as a whole, which in some instances face severe population and economic decline. History, and in particular the long history of national, subnational and more recently supranational government, weighs heavily upon the suburbs of old Europe. European suburbs, in the likes of the Frankfurt and Rhine/Ruhr and South Hampshire areas in Germany and Britain, emerge increasingly as fundamentally in-between places — the unintended consequences of past industrialization and government intervention.[9] Here Europe's *zwischenstadt* places invite imperfect comparisons with and are every bit as unruly as the *desakota* "rurban" fabrics of Indonesia and Japan or the exurban settlements of the United States.[10]

Frankfurt Riedberg, suburban
university expansion (2011)
Source: Roger Keil

While the territoriality of government rarely reflects the dynamics of suburbanization as is the case internationally, nevertheless government profoundly shapes the suburb in this constellation of the modern nation state. In the northern countries of Europe, planning and other machineries of government have been so effective as to virtually eliminate the sorts of impulses to informality and "autoconstruction" still seen in the south. The small, wooden holiday homes that still encourage a seasonal suburbanization in Scandinavia and the small bungalows self-built by Britons across much of the coastal downs of southeast England are now largely consigned to history. Indeed, the bungalow favored by many in Britain as a residential form provides a perfect example of the European suburb as a relay. Imported from India when it was a British colony, it was rapidly reexported to the United States where it became something of the signature of mass, detached, residential suburbia that is only now being reexported to the rest of the rapidly urbanizing world.[11]

It is probably fair to say that we have entered an age of planetary urbanism; of not only a majority of the world's population living in officially defined urban areas, but also, more profoundly, of an even greater majority of the world's population, regardless of where they live, sharing a profoundly urban experience.[12] It is the premise of the global suburbanisms major collaborative research initiative and the sketches in this volume that such planetary urbanism might just as well be regarded as planetary *suburbanism*.

New housing amidst idle land
in Kifissia to the north of Athens
(2004)
Source: Dimitris Ballas

If the European suburban constellation is a guide, it is one that suggests that the suburban world is one of great variety in the agents of change, the pace and timing of that change and the origins and destinations of the multitude of inspirations that drive the production of suburbs and the lived experience within them. The suburban constellation of Europe is one to which we can look for reassurance and also with no little wonder as we navigate a world drawn near in its fundamentally suburban aspect.

Endnotes

1 See Phelps, N.A./Vento, A.T. "Suburban governance in Western Europe." In: Hamel, P. and Keil, R. (eds.): *Suburban Governance: A Global View.* Toronto: University of Toronto Press. 2013.

2 See Maspero, F. *Roissy Express: A Journey Through the Paris Suburbs.* London: Verso. 1994 .
Sage, A. "Tourists Invited for an Eyeful of Gritty Paris Suburbs." In: *The Times.* December 8, 2012. p. 57.

3 Leontidou L./Afouxenidis A./Kourliouros E./Marmaras E. "Infrastructure Related Urban Sprawl: Mega-events and Hybrid Periurban Landscapes in Southern Europe." In: Couch, C./Leontidou, L./Petschel-Held, G. (eds.): *Urban Sprawl in Europe: Landscapes, Land-use Change and Policy.* Oxford: Blackwell. 2007. p. 71–101.

4 Bruegmann, R. Sprawl: A Compact History. Chicago: University of Chicago Press. 2005.

5 Schmid, C. Personal communication, Department of Architecture, ETH (Eidgenössische Technische Hochschule), Zurich.

6 Phelps, N.A./Parsons, N./Ballas, D./Dowling, A. *Post-Suburban Europe: Planning and Politics at the Margins of Europe's Capital Cities.* 2006; Palgrave-MacMillan, B./Røe, P. G. "Green Suburbanisms: Differentiating the Greenness of Suburbs." In: Luccarelli, M./Røe, P. G. (eds.): *Green Oslo: Visions, Planning and Discourse.* Farnham: Ashgate. 2012.

7 Whitehand, J.W.R./Carr, C.M.H. *Twentieth Century Suburbs: A Morphological Approach.* London: Routledge. 2001.

8 Hirt, S. *Iron Curtains: Gates, Suburbs and Privatization of Space in the Post-Socialist City.* Oxford: Blackwell. 2012.
Nuissl, H. /Rink, D. "The 'production' of Urban Sprawl in Eastern Germany as a Phenomenon of Post-Socialist Transition." In: *Cities.* 22. 2005. p. 123–134.

9 Phelps, N.A. *An Anatomy of Sprawl: Planning and Politics in Britain.* London: Routeldge. 2012 & Ludger B. Personal communication. Department of Sociology at Technische Universität Dortmund.

10 Sieverts, T. *Cities Without Cities: An Interpretation of the Zwischenstadt.* London: Routledge. 2003.
McGee, T. "The Emergence of Desakota Regions in Asia." In Ginsborg, N/Koppel, B./ McGee, T. (eds.): *The Extended Metropolis: Settlement Transition in Asia.* Honolulu: University of Hawaii Press. 1991. p. 3–25.

11 Beauregard, R. *America Became Suburban.* Minneapolis: University of Minnesota Press. 2006.

12 Lefebvre, H. *La Révolution Urbaine.* Paris: Gallimard. 1970.

ON CAPITAL'S EDGE: GURGAON, INDIA'S MILLENNIAL CITY

Shubhra Gururani

New Gurgaon (2009)
Source: Shubhra Gururani

In the last two decades, the city of Gurgaon — the so-called Millennial City of India — has captured the imagination of many in India and beyond. Routinely covered not only in the national dailies but also in the columns of international dailies, film documentaries, and photo exhibitions, Gurgaon is considered to be one of the sixteen global cities to watch by none other than Saskia Sassen and Edward Glaeser.[1] As an urban spectacle, Gurgaon is believed to have materialized from "nowhere," a blank space of dust and dirt that has miraculously been transformed against all odds by persuasion, power, and private capital.

Until recently, Gurgaon was considered to be a rural village; a dangerous place of disorder and violence, which marked the agrarian "other" through which the urban and urbane megapolis of Delhi attempted to define and delineate itself. In his autobiography, Mr. K.P. Singh, the CEO of the largest private land developer in Gurgaon — DLF, which initiated the process of land acquisition in the eighties — describes Gurgaon as "a featureless little town in the middle of nowhere, … with large stretches of sparse vegetation and tiny villages dotting the otherwise inhospitable and uninhabited countryside."[2] But, since the late 1980s, Gurgaon has become a prime destination for many multinational corporations, high-end luxury condominiums, BPOs, and more. Its population has gone up almost twenty times, and in a short period of thirty years, agriculture has dropped from 80 to 26 percent of the total land, while the built-up area has increased from 9 to 66 percent.[3]

How this spectacular achievement was accomplished and what complex arrangements of capital, land, property, force, beneficence, patronage, appropriation, and violence made this barren land of dust and dirt materialize into this prized destination is an interesting story but it is not a story of Gurgaon alone. It is a story of the rapid urbanization that is currently underway, especially in the urban peripheries of metropolitan cities in India, and offers a window into the contemporary dynamics of suburban transformation in India.

According to the McKinsey Global Institute Report, India's urban population will be 590 million by 2030. The middle-class population will rise from 22 million to 91 million and there will be 68 cities with over 1 million people; two of the largest five cities in the world will be in India (Mumbai and Delhi). And, the equivalent of a new Chicago each year — 700 to 900 million square meters of commercial and residential space — will be needed to accommodate this urban expansion.[4]

In this moment of immense urban growth, it is important to note that maximum expansion is taking place in the peripheries of metropolitan cities of New Delhi, Mumbai, Kolkata, and Bangalore. Located at the fringes of metropolitan cities, urban peripheries represent a frenzied urbanizing frontier; a rural-urban interface that is typically characterized by mixed land use, intense development, and fragmented pockets of wealth and deprivation. Clearly, like in much of the Global South, in India the process of peri- or suburbanization is also as much about agrarian change as it is about urbanization. In most scenarios, it tends to entail a highly volatile, even violent, process of land acquisition, displacement, and development

High-rise apartments, Gurgaon
(2011)
Source: Shubhra Gururani

Against all odds. High-rise
apartments pop up seemingly
from nowhere (2011)
Source: Shubhra Gururani

Under construction (2012)
Source: Shubhra Gururani

and demonstrates "how varying agrarian structures can create drastically different trajectories of non-agricultural diversification."[5]

In the decades following India's independence in 1947, India's attention was primarily focused on its villages and on food security, infrastructure, and economic development, and the urban question did not figure earnestly in the political discourse. Urban and periurban areas were mostly sleepy towns and villages that were either designated for industrial development or left out from the gaze of planners and policy gurus. In the 1970s — after a turbulent decade of wars, famines, and floods — there was a massive influx of rural migrants to cities, raising questions of urban housing, sanitation, health, transportation, and education. It is during this period that large tracts of land in urban peripheries were acquired for industrial and residential purposes, marking the beginning of suburbanization in India. Starting with the liberalization of the economy in the late 1980s and early 1990s, there was a whole-hearted move toward urbanization through extensive acquisition of agricultural land for residential and commercial purposes and creation of Special Economic Zones specifically for the emerging IT and biotechnology sectors.[6] At this juncture, several land regulations were relaxed and private developers were allowed to acquire large swathes of land at subsidized rates.With land prices skyrocketing, cities became largely unaffordable and led to more and more people moving from cities centers to the peripheries. In this context of suburban boom, even though there were provisions of low-income housing

Property work (2011)
Source: Shubhra Gururani

in these areas, private developers built mainly high-end, posh and all-inclusive housing for the growing middle and upper-middle classes. As a result, with an influx of labor migrants and middle-class families to urban peripheries for work and housing, a complex but visible mosaic of gated communities and slums came to characterize the urban and periurban areas over the last two decades in India.

Several new and old actors played a key role in this process of urban transformation and there consequently is a great deal of diversity in the social and spatial dynamics of periurban areas. But, periurban areas are typically marked by high-density growth and mixed land use and often include "urban villages" nestled with high-rise housing enclaves, shopping malls, golf clubs, biodiversity parks, IT and biotechnology sites, and factories. In this sense, they offer an interesting spatial modality that exceeds easy categorization and necessitate novel ways of seeing and mapping. Since such emergent spaces, especially in the Global South, traverse a wide spectrum of form and processes and are marked by dynamism, fluidity, and contingency, I would argue they demand new vocabularies and categories for analysis, a new set of conceptual anchors that respond to the changing dynamics of class, citizenship, place, and nature that is robustly played out in the spaces of radical urban change in the Global South.

Gurgaon, India's Millennial City, in the district of Gurgaon in Haryana, is one such urban periphery that has undergone rapid urban transformation. Between 2001 and 2011, the district of Gurgaon witnessed a remarkable growth rate of 73.93 per cent and the population density per square kilometer went up from 717 to 1241 during the same decade (2011 Census, Government of India) and the population is expected to grow even further.[7] Located in close proximity to New Delhi, Gurgaon is marked by posh condominiums, shopping malls, and high-rises. It stands as a key articulator in a new and changing regional geography of mobility, networks, and connectivity that increasingly exceed the limits of the nation, and even continents.[8]

In this vista of rapid social and spatial transformation, amidst unmistakable sense of hope and opportunity, Gurgaon however stands as a paradox. On the one hand, it embodies the narrative of India's arrival on the stage of global finance capitalism, a success story in which a former village and rural area stand reformed and transformed in the service of technology and capital. On the other, it is a city besieged by many problems. For example, there are problems of water, transportation, electricity, sanitation, crime, and so on. Despite all these problems and meager infrastructure, land prices continue to rise, and an ever-increasing number of middle- and upper-class residents continue to populate the gated housing enclaves. They do so because they are able to access a range of privatized services through multiple arrangements, while migrant workers live in crammed housing, with little or no access to basic amenities like water, transport, electricity, and health. They make do in a socially, politically, and visually divided and unequal city, which is blatantly comfortable with its unevenness.

Ironically, as more and more bulldozers literally churn Gurgaon inside out and amidst remarkable "deagrarianization,"[9] the discourse of green nature has become a conspicuous referent of a "good life" in Gurgaon. The everyday conversations, images, and advertisements of housing, urban development, and leisure tap into the environmentalist sensibilities and bourgeois desires of the middle classes and evoke nature in countless ways. Developers' descriptions of "green pastoral settings," "lush green surroundings," and "acres of green" are commonplace in Gurgaon. How and why such an aesthetic comes to gain ground and becomes normative over time deserves fuller exploration, and I cannot dwell on it here but I find Louis Mozingo's[10] account of suburban corporate landscape and pastoral capitalism in the United States instructive. Mozingo argues:

> [The] pastoral suburbs proved immensely appealing to upwardly mobile Americans and lucrative to investors. The ongoing advocacy of zealous housing reformers and marketing efforts of speculative real estate developers enthroned leafy residential suburbs as the right and proper environment for a family … By the mid-twentieth century the trenchant correlation of greenness with goodness held sway in American culture.[11]

Indeed some elements of this pastoral capitalism inform the corporate landscape of Gurgaon too, but in a place where villages have not disappeared and pastures are still in the city, the verdant or pastoral landscape indexes a comparable but different sort of relationship with land, nature, and capital. With the opening up of the economy, in order to make Gurgaon palatable and attract corporate capital, private developers actively draw upon the transnational strategy of aestheticizing landscapes through pastoral, verdant motifs, as in the case of American suburbia. But, if land is only another name for nature, which is not produced by man,[12] then the aestheticization of agrarian landscape I would suggest, may be seen as a practice that inscribes class privilege, propriety, access, control, and, more generally, security and safety.

Amidst rapid deagrarianization, the images of verdant landscape in my view not only attempt to make Gurgaon attractive and habitable for residents as well as corporate capital, they also perform another critical role: they work to quell latent skepticism associated with land acquisition and migration and help generate political consensus in a place that is marked by deep inequality. In a fragmented city like Gurgaon, it appears urban nature is enrolled to craft a new geography of suburbs that is not secured through direct exclusion or evacuation but by enactments of private property, propriety, consensus, and moral order. There are subtle and sometimes not so subtle exclusions that run along multiple indexes of difference but those of class, caste, gender and ethnicity stand out. Importantly, such claims over basic resources are not taking place only at the behest of state priorities but are steered by curious and contingent alliances of local and non-local actors. These include citizen groups, who under the patronage of the state and capital work to generate new configurations of land and property, depoliticize the environment, and push the mandate of private property and more broadly further neoliberalism in unprecedented ways.

In such a context of emerging urban and suburban constellations of society and nature, it is therefore critical to acknowledge the highly contested dynamics of urban transformation and entertain the possibilities of imagining cities and societies that are socially and environmentally just. In order to do so, it is necessary that we simultaneously attend to the politics of social *and* natural processes and seek an ecological understanding of capitalist urbanization and transformation that is tending towards consumption, appropriation, and accumulation.

Endnotes

1   Sasken, S./Glaeser, E. 2011. *16 Global Cities to Watch.* http://www.foreignpolicy.com/articles/2011/11/28/16_global_cities_to_watch#, 06.02.13.

2   Singh, K.P. *Whatever the Odds: The Incredible Story Behind DLF.* (With Menon, R./Swamy, R.). New Delhi: HarperCollins. 2011. p.180–181.

3   See Gupta, R./S. Nangia. "Population Explosion and Land Use Changes in Gurgaon City, a Satellite of Delhi." Paper presented at the International Union for the Scientific Study of Population XXV International; Population Conference, Paris, France, July 18–23, 2005.

4   "India's Urban Awakening: Building Inclusive Cities, Sustaining Economic Growth." McKinsey Global Institute. April 2010.

5   Roy, A. *City Requiem, Calcutta: Gender and the Politics of Poverty.* Minneapolis: University of Minnesota Press. 2003. p. 15.

6   Dupont, V. "Conflicting Stakes and Governance in the Peripheries of Large Indian Metropolises: An Introduction." In *Cities.* 2007. 24(2). p. 89–94.

7   2011 Census. Ministry of Home Affairs. Government of India.

8   Mbembe, A./S. Nuttal. "Writing the World from an African Metropolis" In: *Public Culture.* 2004. 16 (3). p. 347–372.

9   Hall, D./Hirsch, P./Li, TM. *Powers of Exclusion: Land Dilemmas in Southeast Asia.* National University of Singapore. Singapore. 2005. They describe deagrarianization as "the process by which agriculture becomes progressively less central to national economies and the livelihoods of people in even rural areas." p. 1.

10 Mozingo, L. *Pastoral Capitalism: A History of Suburban Corporate Landscape.* MIT Press. 2011.

11 Ibid., p. 11.

12 Polanyi, Karl. *The Great Transformation: The Political and Economic Origins of our Time.* Beacon Press. Boston. 1944.

CHINESE SUBURBAN CONSTELLATIONS: THE GROWTH MACHINE, URBANIZATION, AND MIDDLE-CLASS DREAMS

Fulong Wu

Suburban expansion, Shanghai.
The view from Pudong (2006)
Source: Roger Keil

The "suburb" in Chinese language is *jiaoqu*, or literally, sub-district; it refers to the places near the city, in a geographical sense and does not imply a distinctive type of settlement or a category of residence.

The meaning of "suburbia" has been absent in the Chinese context. The image of Chinese suburbia is different from the American stereotype of a single-family, middle-class residence amidst urban sprawl. In fact, the divide in Chinese society is not urban-versus-suburban but rather an urban-rural dualism. The urban and rural systems are distinctively different, characterized by two profoundly different types of citizenship and administrative mechanisms. The urban is a state-led industrial society built upon cellular organizations known as *danwei* (work units), while the rural has been left largely as a self-contained under-developed society. This dualism has been under transformation since China opened its doors to the world and began to build itself into the "world's factory."

The suburbs are where this reconstruction is happening, at the intersections between the urban and rural areas: millions of rural migrants move to the city but instead of landing in the central areas, they find rental accommodation in the suburbs. The suburbs thus witness dramatic spatial constellation in the process of Chinese urbanization. To review this process, we should trace the changes back through the era of state-planned economy.

Until the early 1980s, the suburbs of Chinese cities were largely countryside. Among the vast hinterland of large metropolises were scattered a few state industrial districts or industrial satellite towns usually based on key state projects. The suburbs were under-developed and remained rural areas to which residents were reluctant to be relocated. Spontaneous residential moves were rare, often associated with job and housing allocation to these industrial sites. Because of the under-developed facilities and lower quality of schools, the suburbs were not attractive places. Some were developed purposely through city plans as "anti-magnetic" poles to decentralize population, but in reality these projects were largely unsuccessful. This is very different from the American connotation of suburbs as the place for a more desirable single-family life.

Before the economic reform that began in 1979, Chinese cities were quite compact. The dominant commuting modes were cycling and walking, and due to the close association between workplace and housing (provided as occupational welfare), the differentiation of residence and workplace was not significant. Public resources and facilities were concentrated in congested central areas with very high densities. The establishment of housing markets changed the preference for a central location by introducing a price factor. A suburban location was cheaper and more spacious. For the first time, Chinese urban residents began to see suburban estates as alternative places to live.

Along with rising income, there was a strong desire to improve housing conditions. Since then, large estates built through "commodity housing development" have been developed in the Chinese suburbs, targeting different consumer groups. For most of the urban population, residential relocation is an effective way to find larger housing space and improve living conditions. Residential relocation is also driven by the redevelopment of central cities, where old neighborhoods are demolished to make space for office and commercial buildings and high-end housing. Many residents may be relocated through urban redevelopment projects rather than their own choosing.

No matter whether relocating to the suburbs is due to one's own preference or influenced by redevelopment, the suburb is no longer a subsidiary category but becoming a mainstream residential location. In short, the Chinese suburb now becomes the new frontier of China's urban development.

In terms of built form, it is characterized by high-rise apartments built in master-planned estates rather than terraced and detached houses and villas. The density is comparably much higher than what is seen in the sprawling suburbs of North America. The appearance of Chinese suburbs is similar to those housing estates in Hong Kong and new towns in Singapore. Gated communities are the norm rather than exception. In the upper-market gated compounds, villas and detached houses are usually for the new rich.

Many buy these properties as an investment and use them as the second or third home. Some gated residences deliberately adopt an alien/Western landscape and brand them with foreign place names to satisfy the imagination of their owners for an elite and ostentatious style of consumption. For example, the Thames Town of Shanghai tries to mimic the style of English market town,[1] while the estates like Napa Valley and Orange County in Beijing boast their "authentic" California design.[2]

Compared with traditional neighborhoods, these new estates place greater emphasis on privacy and security features. This aims to suit the residents' desire to reduce all-inclusive and close social relations in danwei communities and live in a more private environment. In the gated communities, services are purchased from and managed by property management companies rather than from workplaces or departments of the local government. Homeowners' associations play an important role in the appointment of the property management company and the management of community affairs. In contrast to orderly planned commodity housing areas, urban informality is another outstanding feature in new suburbs.[3]

In the periurban areas, former villages were engulfed by rapid urban expansion. To save on the cost of land acquisition, the sites of villages were deliberately left out while the farmland nearby was turned into industrial and urban uses. These rural villages thus became "urban villages" or "villages in the city" (chengzhongcun). Because the land is assigned to individual households, under the condition of relatively lax rural land management, rural farmers began to extend their houses and become landlords of rental housing for migrants who tried hard to find accommodation in the city. The urban villages thus become the habitat for rural migrants in urban China.[4] Despite their under-developed facilities, urban villages represent a more human living environment for rural migrants than factory-managed dormitory housing, because over 60 percent of migrants in the villages bring in their families and have a normal family life rather than sharing rooms in dormitories. The habitat of urban villages is threatened by the bulldozers of redevelopment programs and is transient and short-lived, giving way soon to more formal master-planned estates. However, the constellation of formality and informality does not disappear — more informal settlements soon appear upon the influx of rural migrants and the relocation of existing migrant population from the demolished settlements to other rural villages.

Under state socialism, suburban development was for a long time driven by state industrial projects and was a burden to the local government. The mechanism has changed along with the development of state entrepreneurialism[5] and the changing business model of local government. Rather than becoming a financial burden, suburbs opened up a new space for land development, generating revenue for the local government. Through economic devolution, local governments have been given more responsibilities for social expenditures. The tax sharing system between the central and local governments, however, concentrates the tax revenue with the central government. As a result, there is a significant gap in revenue and expenditure and most local governments run on a fiscal deficit. However, the system also allows the local government to retain the profit from land sales. To make up the fiscal gap, local governments have begun to use their power in compulsory land purchases to acquire the land from farmers, develop it into serviced land, and then release it to investors.

Local governments are willing to sell the land at a lower or heavily subsidized price to the manufacturing sector in the hopes of boosting the local economy. The local government can then sell the land nearby at a much higher price to property developers, which eventually brings in a profit through suburban land development.

In response to the changing business model of local government, the mode of suburban governance has shifted from a managerial style to the "entrepreneurial local state." Development zones and new towns are established and managed by business-oriented committees. Some have been created by breaking existing jurisdictional units and reassembling part of them into new, cross-boundary development zones. The initial management is streamlined, focusing on attracting investment and infrastructure provision. This is less a layer of government and more like a development corporation. However, with the increase in population size and complex functions, the demand for social services increases.

For example, one important challenge facing many industrial zones is the provision of affordable housing to key workers. The imbalance of work and residential uses constrains the operation of these industrial zones. The housing for their workers is largely left to the informal market to provide rentals. The development zone corporation often has to negotiate with nearby local governments for providing necessary services. When the suburban industrial zone is growing into a new town, its corporate style of governance has to evolve into a full local government. And indeed in places such as the Beijing Economic and Technological Development Zone, this is happening. For example the new town of Yizhuang is formed as one major new city in-between Beijing and Tianjin metropolises. When this happens, the suburb grows out of its monotonic residential or industrial function and becomes part of the city — in a sense this is becoming "post-suburbia."[6]

In less than two decades, the Chinese city has been turned inside out; the suburb has become the fast-growing area. But this spatial reconfiguration is not a Los Angeles style of post-Fordist edge growth, though it is possible to find out some elements such as LA-inspired gated communities in the Chinese suburbs.

Chinese suburban development is more about constellations of urbanization and suburbanization, and it is heterogeneous in terms of population composition. Growth has been driven by the relocation of local farmers, rural-urban migration and the out-movement of urban residents from central districts. The process is quite different from the "white flight" and the formation of relatively homogenous affluent middle-class residential areas in the US[7] and there are different motivations.

For the new rich, changing consumption behavior is certainly behind their pursuit of a suburban dream, while a less affluent working population is either pushed out by inflated house prices or relocated through urban redevelopment. For rural migrants, the inner suburbs provide access to jobs while minimizing living costs. While the development of suburban land-based "growth machine" is part of explanation for rapid land requisition and conversion, the consumption-side explanation is becoming more and more responsible for the differentiation between white-collar and migrant suburbs and differentiation between apartments and villas.[8] For example, high-density apartments are less associated with the distinct suburban life and more with the provision of affordable housing along mass transit to access the central core, while villa compounds are chosen for their exclusive services, quality amenities, and enchanting living environments.

Migrant workers come from the countryside or other small towns to work in the suburbs of large Chinese cities. At the same time, the local governments promote industrial development and development zones in these places. Now, we begin to see a result of "urbanization of suburbs" in addition to the residential-driven suburban development built to suit middle-class dreams.

Endnotes

1   Shen, J./ Wu, F. "The Development of Master-Planned Communities in Chinese Suburbs: A Case Study of Shanghai's Thames Town. *Urban Geography.* 33(2). 2012. p. 183–203.

2   Wu, F. "Gated and Packaged Suburbia: Packaging and Branding Chinese Suburban Residential Development." In: *Cities.* 27(5). 2010. p. 385–396.

3   Wu, F./ Zhang, F./Webster, C. "Informality and the Development and Demolition of Urban Villages in the Chinese Periurban Area. In: *Urban Studies.* 2013, forthcoming.

4   Wu, F./ Zhang, F./Webster, C . *Rural Migrants in Urban China: Enclaves and Transient Urbanism.* Abingdon, Oxon: Routledge. 2013.

5   Wu, F./ Phelps, N. 2011. "(Post)Suburban Development and State Entrepreneurialism in Beijing's Outer Suburbs." In: *Environment and Planning A.* 43(2). 2011. p. 410–430.

6   Ibid.

7   Beauregard, R. *When America Became Suburban.* Minneapolis: University of Minnesota Press. 2006.

8   Shen, J./ Wu, F. Moving to the Suburbs: Demand-Side Driving Forces of Suburban Growth in China. In: *Environment and Planning A.* 2013, forthcoming.

DESIRE, DRYNESS, AND DECADENCE: LIVING BIG IN AUSTRALIA'S SUBURBS

Louise C. Johnson

"House in the sky": a sculpture commissioned by Melbourne's western suburban councils on a major freeway interchange (2009). Designed by Brearley Middleton Architects and erected in 2002, it is "an accurate rendering of the surrounding mansions". Source: Murray McCrae

There are (at least!) two remarkable things about Australia: one is that it is the driest inhabited continent on the planet and the second that it has the largest houses in the world. The relationship between these two facts serves as one way of understanding its settlement patterns and the character of its suburbs, foregrounding the desires that underpin their cultural economies.

For a country where three-quarters of its landmass is either arid or semi-arid, it is no surprise that more than 80 percent of Australia's population lives within fifty kilometers of the better watered coast and over 65 percent inhabit the major cities hugging the coastline.[1] Such cities were the original entry points for the colonizing British. A key element of resulting conflict with the Indigenous population was access to water as stolen lands were carved into pastoral runs fronting the few permanent rivers and non-indigenous animals drank and fouled the limited surface water. Many an intrepid explorer subsequently ventured in search of the fabled inland sea, only to die of thirst alongside the Indigenes who could tap into plants or underground to the artesian oceans that lay below.[2] But it was not to the bush that the immigrant masses would venture, but to the coastal strip encircling much of the continent. And it was in the coastal towns, created at a critical juncture in the shift from mercantilism to manufacturing, that the activities of traders, financiers, bureaucrats and then industrialists were to cluster. In these cities, expansive suburbs were envisaged from the earliest days of occupation.

Surveying the first European settlement, British Governor Arthur Phillip required that Sydney's 1798 streets: "afford the free circulation of air, and when the houses are built … the land will be granted with a clause that will prevent more than one being built on the allotment, which will be sixty feet in front and one hundred and fifty in depth."[3] Australia's white founders anticipated a city of free-standing houses with spacious gardens, rather than the replication of London's terraces and alleys. It was to be a land of suburbs, where water was lavished on expansive gardens and supplied as needed to the homes of the wealthy and the temperate.

This walking city, until the spread of tram and railways in the 1880s, was distinguished by the rich living close to the city center, a middle class living in purely residential suburbs on the elevated edges of the city, and office and factory workers living near their work, either in the city center, around the port or in industrial working class suburbs with their dense mixture of factories, warehouses, pubs and shops.[4] As trade and industry grew and the urban land markets boomed, these city centers became increasingly cluttered places of disorder, dirt, disease, and the less desirable. As the harbors and rivers fouled with the detritus of the urban and industrial population, movement beyond the city by the well to do to places of elevation, cleanliness, safety, and morality accelerated. It was to be the pestilence and disease emanating from the inner-city dwellings and activities that also forced the provision by colonial governments of reticulated water supplies and the building of elaborate sewerage systems within Australian cities. Such systems, along with the large households — averaging

4.5 people — and lavish gardens of the suburban middle classes, meant that per capita water consumption doubled from the mid-century level of 100 liters per person, per day, to 200 liters in 1890.[5] The march towards massive urban water consumption and its technologically mediated provision had begun, replacing moderation and self-provision. The backyard water tank, along with the vegetable patch and home-based food production, remained for the working classes. But for the middle and upper classes, these were now things of the past. The humble water tank, was soon rendered illegal, supposedly to ensure water quality but mainly to prop up the economics of large, centralized systems.

If Australia was born urban and quickly became suburban over the nineteenth century, it was the proliferation of private car ownership, provision of finance and the long economic boom after World War II that triggered the spatial explosion of its cities and the democratization of suburbanization. Along with its sprawling suburbs went a huge expansion in per capita water consumption — to 400 liters per person per day in the 1950s — as the detached house on its large quarter-acre block reached its zenith. However, though water consumption was vast, house sizes were not. Australia's suburban house was modeled on the British cottager and while it moved from being a two-room to a four- or six-roomed dwelling across the nineteenth century, for the majority it had never been a particularly large dwelling. Such modest dimensions continued with the 1920s Californian bungalow and they in turn were curtailed by the 1930s Depression and by postwar scarcity and austerity. While home ownership rates peaked at 71 percent in 1961, it was to be the size of houses rather than their ownership that became the remarkable element of Australian suburbs thereafter. For as affluence rose and spread across the social spectrum, so did the size of houses. Thus in 1984, the average Australian home had 150 square meters of floor space , while in 2008–09 it had grown to 253 square meters; the largest in the world! At the same time, the average block of land decreased in size (from the much lauded half acre or 1,012 square meters in the 1970s, to 800 square meters in 1993–94, and to 735 square meters in 2003–04). The number of people actually living in each dwelling also fell, from close to four people in the middle of the twentieth century to 2.6 in 2011.[6] The vast and much maligned McMansion captured so well by the *House in the Sky*, a sculpture perched alongside a Melbourne highway, became all too typical in twenty-first century Australian suburbs.

As houses got bigger, so did water consumption: peaking in Melbourne at 500 liters per person per day and in Brisbane at a staggering 700 liters per person per day in the mid-1990s. Households consume 60 percent of Melbourne's water. While the laundry and bathroom use 70 percent, another 25 percent is used outdoors, primarily to water the gardens of suburban houses. Such figures vary by state and city, relating both to climate and to historical regulatory regimes, but overall the pattern is of massive water consumption by fewer people in larger houses. The image of a dripping tap at one of the newer outer suburban developments in Melbourne's west is indicative of such a pattern.

To explain such a divergence in this parched continent, it is necessary to acknowledge the changing structural regime since the 1990s, which has seen the privatization and corporatization of the nineteenth- and early twentieth-century state water authorities, but also to engage with the role of desire in the valuing and use of water. For as Graeme Davison points out in his historical examination of Australia's water use, the structural and technical elements of supply are but one part of the story, what is also critical are notions of health, purity, dirt, and morality.[7] Changing notions of personal hygiene and the deployment of swimming pools have been vital in the growth of water consumption. It is not just the suburban house form that is implicated in this story, but the particular suburban life style that has emerged in Australia in the last thirty years.

Davison tracks the importance of abundant hot water as a key technical development that allowed more regular bathing, but the introduction of water guzzling washing machines and dishwashers drove growing per capita water consumption over the late twentieth century. Thus in 1943, only 2 percent of Melbourne's houses had hot water service; a problem that had disappeared by the 1960s when all urban Australian families had access to unlimited amounts of hot water with which to bathe, cook, and clean. The movement of the bath from an infrequently used copper dish located outside, to something present in at least two if not three bathrooms within the home, has been a major contributor to the rise in water usage. Such a change has been associated with very different conceptions of personal hygiene and the beautification of the body. From preoccupations with health and safety in the nineteenth century, the bathroom it is now associated with sexualized notions of pampering within the McMansions of Australian suburbia.

But if desire, not only for groomed bodies but for lots of clean clothes and outdoor swimming pools and spas has led to an explosion in water usage, the realities of ongoing urban population growth, intense droughts, and a long-term decline in rainfall over south eastern Australia, has led to a radical rethink of such patterns. From a high of 500 liters per person per day, Melbournians now consume 250 liters per person per day (in 2009). Governments had responded to a nationwide, decade-long drought to impose increasingly tough water usage restrictions, and funded educational campaigns to lower consumption levels. These demand-management strategies were accompanied by a host of technological fixes to increase the supply of urban water. In Melbourne the push was on to get individuals to consume no more than 155 liters per day, but also to line irrigation channels, create a state wide water grid, recommission old dams, and build a huge desalination plant. While desalination was embraced by anxious state governments across Australia, the largest — at a costs of A$3.2 billion — will produce 17 percent of Melbourne's supply. Built as a public-private partnership with a French multinational at the height of the drought, its costly waters are now superfluous, but have to be taken and also paid for by massive increases in costs to users.

While Big Water has been enhanced, individuals and households have embraced the challenge of consuming less water, accepting subsidies to install dual flush toilets and low flow shower heads, recycled gray water, reintroduced water tanks and so on; while suburban developers also installed third pipe water reticulation systems, pondage and other runoff minimization and reuse systems as both marketing ploys and conservation measures. The dripping tap is therefore ironically representative of the issues such measures addressed, a new appreciation of the value of water, and the problems of its wastage. So indeed, per capita water consumption has declined dramatically as desire has been recalibrated, while the investment in water supplies has increased equally dramatically.

What does all of this mean now for a suburban landscape that was produced at a time of water abundance? At least three contradictory things are occurring: ongoing household water conservation via the techno fixes in appliances as well as in major changes in garden forms, sizes, and uses; along with a genuine commitment by many to use less, be more self-sufficient and decentralize water, energy and food provision; expensive over-investment in technologically provided solutions in desalination plants and improved irrigation schemes; and an ongoing demand for suburban space as house sizes continue to grow along with the demand for water via bathrooms, spas, pools, showers … such that Australia's water footprint remains the world's largest, along with the size of its suburban houses.

Endnotes

1   Australian Government. State of Australian Cities Report, Major Cities Unit, Infrastructure Australia, Canberra: Australian Government. 2010.

2   Cathcart, M. *The Water Dreamers: The Remarkable History of Our Dry Continent*. Melbourne: Text Publishing. 2009.

3   Davison, G. "The Past and Future of the Australian Suburb." In: Johnson, L.C. (ed.): *Suburban Dreaming: An Interdisciplinary Approach to Australian Cities*. Geelong: Deakin University Press. 1999. p. 99–113.

4   McCarty, J. "Australian Capital Cities in the 19th Century." In: *Australian Economic History Review*. 1977. 10. p. 107–137.

5   Davison, G. "Down the Gurgler: Historical Influences on Australian Water Consumption." In Troy, P. (ed.): *Troubled Waters: Confronting the Water Crisis in Australian Cities*. Canberra: ANU E-press. 2008.

6   Australian Bureau of Statistics. 2011. www.environment.gov.au. 12.12.12.

7   On the association of clean bodies with virtue, see Douglas, M. *Purity and Danger*. London: Routledge. 1966 & Kegan, P. On the cultural economy of water supply and consumption, see Soufoulis, Z. "Big Water, Everyday Water: A Sociotechnical Perspective." In: *Continuum: Journal of Media and Culture*. 19(4). 2005. p. 445-63 and Allon, F./Soufoulis, Z. "Everyday Water: Cultures in Transition." In: *Australian Geographer*. 37(1). 2006. p. 45–55.

ESCAPE FROM THE BURBS?

Roger Keil

Foreclosure Center,
Palmdale California (2012)
Source: Roger Keil

Let's take a drive through the sprawl
Through these towns they built to change
And then you said "The emotions are dead"
It's no wonder that you feel so estranged
The last defender of the sprawl
Said "Well, where do you kids live?"
Well, sir, if you only knew what the answer's worth
Been searching every corner of the earth ...

Arcade Fire, "Sprawl I (Flatland)," from *The Suburbs*, 2010

This book has presented a kaleidoscope of suburban experiences. We used a critical (re)view of the literature, of the (sub)urban forms, of the ways of life we find around the world in the peripheries of the urban revolution. We started in New York City, the most urbanized place on the planet, so it seemed. On our journey, we have horizontalized the image of the urban landscape. We are, to employ the title of the Arcade Fire song in the opening quote, in the "flatland" of the suburban experience, have defied centers, have identified life in the sprawl. We now begin to know and accept that this life exists most anywhere we see the urban revolution proceed around the globe.

To arrive in the global suburb is no longer an original experience. It is not terra incognita, empty unmarked space. The moving trucks taking the huddled masses to the air and light of the periphery have long disappeared. Arriving in the suburb is getting home to the metropolitan future that is most likely ours for some time to come. The authors and artists who present their work in this book are neither apologists for the limitless consumption of land that undergirds the production of suburban space worldwide; nor are they falling in line with the kneejerk chorus against all things suburban. The contributions to this volume are measured interventions into a debate that will be with us in future decades: how do we live in our post-suburban future now that we have made it?

There are things to learn from past urbanization processes, but there will also be new surprises. While land seemed endless for a while, it cannot be produced at will. While infrastructural and technological solutions appeared "ready-to-wear" for every new turn in the urban revolution, we now need smarter solutions that are resilient and sustainable at once. While governance helped us produce the suburbs, we now need forms of governance that assist us in figuring out how to live in them with their diversity, their aging built environments and exploding mobility, cultural, and social needs.

There is no escape from the burbs. Like the kids in the Arcade Fire's "Sprawl," suburban populations will evolve, move and disappear, only to show up again in some other corner of global suburbia. We have arrived in the heart of the suburban revolution.

CONTRIBUTORS

ROBIN BLOCH is a professionally-trained Urban and Regional Planner with over 20 years of international professional/practitioner experience in urban, metropolitan and regional planning, spatial and land use planning, urban and regional economic development, and urban environmental planning and management. He is the Principal Consultant for GHK Consulting. His work has incorporated the full spectrum of the project cycle from project identification and formulation through implementation, quality assurance and the monitoring and evaluation of individual projects and programs. He also has long-run international experience of policymaking and of urban, regional and economic development strategy and planning, at local, regional and national government levels. Bloch is also research affiliate at the University of the Witwatersrand and the University of Cape Town. Most recently he published "Dubai's long goodbye" in the International Journal of Urban and Regional Research.

KATERINA CIZEK is an Emmy-winning documentary filmmaker working across many media platforms. Her work has documented the Digital Revolution, and has itself become part of the movement. Her current digital project at the National Film Board of Canada is called *HIGHRISE*, exploring the human condition in vertical suburbs. Recently, she was listed as one of Reelscreen's 2011 Trailblazers in Non-Fiction. For five years, she was the National Film Board of Canada's Filmmaker-in-Residence at an inner-city hospital, in a many-media project that won a 2008 Webby Award ("The Internet's Oscars"), a Banff Award, and a Canadian New Media Award. Her previous award-winning films include *Seeing is Believing: Handicams, Human Rights and*

the News (2002, co-directed with Peter Wintonick). She teaches and presents around the world about her innovative approach to the documentary genre.

FEIKE DE JONG is a writer, journalist, researcher, photographer, and urbanist in Mexico City. In 2010 he won the Walter Reuter prize for best article on climate change in Mexican media. In 2009 he undertook a 51-day expedition on foot around the edge of Mexico City. His principle research interest is sustainable development and auto-poiesis on the spatial edges of megalopoli in developing countries and Mexico City in particular.

Teaching at York University, **LISA DRUMMOND'S** research focuses primarily on urban social life in Vietnam, including analyses of public space, popular culture, and women's roles in Vietnamese society. Her publications include several co-edited books, most recently *The Reinvention of Distinction: Modernity and the Modern Class in Urban Vietnam* with Van Nguyen-Marshall and Danièle Bélanger, as well as *Consuming Urban Culture in Contemporary Vietnam*, with Mandy Thomas, and *Gender Practices in Contemporary Vietnam*, with Helle Rydstrøm. Professor Drummond is engaged in research on several ongoing projects: *Socialist Cities in the 21ˢᵗ Century* (with Doug Young), *Water in the City: Community Participation and Water Access in Southeast Asian Cities* (with Amrita Danière), and the Global Suburbanisms MCRI (led by Roger Keil). Professor Drummond is currently writing a book about public space in Hanoi from the French colonial period to the present, and preparing a co-edited (with Helle Rydstrøm) volume on fieldwork in Vietnam in the early 1990s.

PIERRE FILION'S recent research work focuses on the obstacles to a smart growth inspired transformation of cities, as well as metropolitan scale planning models put forth in the plans of large North American metropolitan regions. More generally, his research projects have dealt with the relationship between transportation and land use, and with the impact of societal change on cities with a particular focus on values, the economy and institutions. More specific areas of research include downtowns, the changing structure of metropolitan regions, and suburban centers

SHUBHRA GURURANI is Associate Professor of Social Anthropology and Associate Director of the York Center of Asian Research at York University, Canada. Her research lies at the intersection of political ecology and science and technology studies and ethnographically explores the everyday practices of gender, place work, and care through which nature is made and remade. She is currently studying the politics of urbanization, sewage, and urban natures in periurban India, with a focus on the Millennial City – Gurgaon in the outskirts of New Delhi. Her papers have been published in *Journal of Peasant Studies, International Journal of Social Sciences, Gender, Place, and Culture*. Her previous work focused on the politics of conservation, history of forestry and social movements in the Indian Himalayas.

PIERRE HAMEL is sociology professor at Université de Montréal and the editor of the sociology journal 'Sociologie et sociétés'. His research interests focus on three themes: 1) urban issues, urban development and urban policies; 2) collective action, democracy and social justice; 3) modernity and the capacity of urban Institutions to regulate economic and social inequalities. He has written extensively on social movements, urban politics, governance and local democracy. Hamel's most recent publication, written with Louis Guay, is *Cities and Urban Sociology* (Oxford University Press, forthcoming). During the academic year of 2010 – 2011, he was the holder of the Chair on Canadian Studies at Paris 3 – Sorbonne Nouvelle.

RICHARD HARRIS teaches urban historical geography at McMaster University, Canada. A Fellow of the Royal Society of Canada and recipient of Fulbright and Guggenheim Fellowships, he has published on the building industry, housing, housing policy, and suburban development in North America and the British colonies. His most recent book is *Building a Market. The Rise of the Home Improvement Industry,* 1914-1960 (Chicago, 2012)

DIRK HEINRICHS currently coordinates a DLR research initiative on Transport and the Environment. Between 2005 and 2010, he led the Risk Habitat Megacity project, a collaboration of the German Helmholtz Association, universities in Latin America and the UN ECLAL with a focus on urban sustainable development in the region. His research focuses on the governance of suburban development in Latin America and Europe. Dirk is also working on urban adaptation to climate change. In this capacity, he is a member of several climate networks such as the Urban Climate Change Research Network (UCCRN) and the Urbanization and Global Environmental Change (UGEC) core project of the International Human Dimensions Programme (IHDP). Heinrichs' recent publications include "Urban Sprawl and New Challenges for (Metropolitan) Governance in Latin America – the Case of Santiago de Chile" (*Revista* EURE), with Henning Nuissl and Claudia Rodriguez Seeger,

and "Fresh Wind or Hot Air? Does the Governance Discourse Have Something to Offer to Spatial Planning?" (*Journal of Planning Education and Research*), co-authored with Henning Nuissl.

SEAN HERTEL is a Toronto-based urban planner with experience in policy formulation and development both inside and outside the city. Sean is a Member of the Canadian Institute of Planners, is a Registered Professional Planner in the province of Ontario, and holds a Master in Environmental Studies degree from York University. Sean has conducted academic research on suburban ways of life, and continues that work through his role as Coordinator of the Greater Toronto Suburban Working Group housed at the City Institute at York University.

LOUISE C. JOHNSON is Professor in Australian Studies. A human geographer, she has researched the gendered nature of suburban houses and shopping centre, changing manufacturing workplaces as well as the dynamics of Australian regional economies. Major publications include *Suburban Dreaming* (DUP 1994) and *Placebound: Australian Feminist Geographies* (OUP 2000). Her most recent work has examined Geelong, Bilbao, Singapore and Glasgow as *Cultural Capitals* (Ashgate 2009) looking at how the arts have been re-valued and urban spaces remade by the creative economy. She is currently researching the nature of master planned suburban communities and post-colonial planning.

ROGER KEIL teaches at the Faculty of Environmental Studies at York University, Toronto and is the Principal Investigator of Global Suburbanisms. He is the co-editor (with Pierre Hamel) of *Suburban Governance: A Global View* (UTP) and author of the forthcoming *Global Suburbs* (Polity). He previously published *In-between Infrastructure: Urban Connectivity in an Age of Vulnerability* (ed. with Douglas Young and Patricia Burke Wood, Praxis(e) Press, 2011); *Changing*

Toronto: Governing the Neoliberal City (with Julie-Anne Boudreau and Douglas Young; UTP 2009); *Networked Disease: Emerging Infections and the Global City.* (ed. with S.Harris Ali; Wiley-Blackwell, 2008); *Leviathan Undone? The Political Economy of Scale.* (ed. with Rianne Mahon, UBC Press 2009) and *The Global Cities Reader* (ed. with Neil Brenner; Routledge, 2006).

DANIELLE LABBÉ'S research is focused on understanding how rapidly urbanizing territories in Vietnam become both strategic resources for government interventions and sites of local resistance to those interventions and to the discourses they embody. Her ongoing research projects look at the production and appropriation of new town developments on the outskirts of Hanoi and at land conflicts in the Red River delta region. Danielle Labbé speaks Vietnamese and undertakes regular research trips to Hanoi where she collaborates with scholars at leading research institutes and universities. She has recently published articles in *Pacific Affairs, International Development and Planning Review* and *CyberGeo: European Journal of Geography.*

UTE LEHRER holds a PhD in Urban Planning from UCLA. She taught at SUNY Buffalo and Brock University before joining York, where she is an Associate Professor in the Faculty of Environmental Studies. She has been involved in comparative urban research on Zurich, Frankfurt, Berlin, Los Angeles and Toronto, investigating new urban forms, processes of spectacularization and megaprojects. She has recently completed a SSHRC-funded project on "Urban Images, Public Space and the Growth of Private Interest in Toronto" in which she studied the development of private residential real estate development in form of condominium towers in Toronto and is currently heading a comparative study of suburban identities in the Frankfurt and Toronto regions.

ALAN MABIN is a professor at the School of Architecture and Planning, University of the Witwatersrand, Johannesburg. Alan completed his doctorate at Simon Fraser University, Canada (1984) and is a Corporate Member of the South African Planning Institute. His urban development experience includes urban NGO work particularly with Planact which he helped to found in 1985, as well as public sector consulting (since 1994). He was Deputy Chairperson, national Development and Planning Commission, 1997-2000. Alan has spent time at Yale University, USA (1987-88), Queen's University, Canada (1995), Institut Universitaire de France (2003), Université de Paris Ouest-Nanterre-La Défense and Ardhi University, Dar es Salaam (both on several occasions), Laboratoire Architecture Ville Urbanisme Environnement (CNRS UMR 7218) 2010-11, Universidade de São Paulo (2011) and Sciences Po Paris (2013).

CLAIRE MAJOR is a PhD Candidate in the Department of Geography and a Resident PhD Student at the CITY Institute, York University. Her dissertation is on socially reproducing workers in Fort McMurray, Alberta. Major's interests include theorizing social reproduction at the scale of the city, qualitative methodologies, post-Fordist labour relationships, political ecology, post-post modernism, interpreting community, and urban growth and governance. In 2013, she and T. Winters co-authored "Community by necessity: Security, insecurity, and the flattering of class in Fort McMurray, Alberta", which will be published in the Canadian *Journal of Sociology*.

STEPHEN MAK is a practicing architect whose practice centres around developments in largely under developed suburban sites throughout Canada. A graduate of the University of Waterloo, in addition to practicing architecture he is an avid photographer having retaken up the craft that began at a young age.

TERRY MCGEE is Professor Emeritus at the University of British Columbia, (Vancouver). Throughout his research career of more than 50 years, Terry McGee has focused on the urbanization process in Asia, particularly in Southeast Asia. He published more than 40 books. reports and monographs and over 200 articles. McGee is now carrying out research on regional sustainable development in urbanizing regions of Malaysia and Indonesia.

PABLO MENDEZ is a Post-Doctoral Fellow in the Department of Geography at the University of British Columbia, Canada. His doctoral dissertation examined the informal housing practice of renting illegally built apartments inside single-family houses, focusing on the inner suburbs of the city of Vancouver. Pablo has also been involved in several projects investigating the relationship between housing and immigration in Canada's metropolitan areas.

JOCHEN MONSTADT is professor and head of the working group for spatial and infrastructure planning at Darmstadt University of Technology, Germany. His research interests are at the interface between urban/regional studies and social studies of technology. He has conducted and coordinated extensive international research on the urban transition of energy, water and wastewater systems, on the co-evolution of cities and infrastructures and on infrastructure planning and urban governance.

MARKUS MOOS is an Assistant Professor in the School of Planning at the University of Waterloo, Canada. He studies the changing economies and social structures of cities, particularly the implications for sustainability and equity of housing, location and commute patterns. His current research focuses on local labour market restructuring and Canada's changing suburbs, and the implications for public policy and planning. He has published on these topics in book

chapters, national and international journals and news articles.

JAN NIJMAN is Professor of Urban Studies and director of the Centre for Urban Studies at the University of Amsterdam. Most of his work deals with urban theory and the role of cities in their broader regional and historical contexts. Widely published, his regional expertise is in North America and South Asia, with special interests in Miami and Mumbai. His most recent book is Miami: Mistress of the Americas, University of Pennsylvania Press, 2011.

HENNING NUISSL is Professor of Applied Geography and Town Planning at the Humboldt-Universität zu Berlin. He held guest professorships at Technische Universität Berlin and Potsdam University. His areas of interest include urban sprawl and land use change, regional development, and urban and regional governance.

OGINO:KNAUSS is a collective of architects and artists dealing with urban exploration and innovative representation forms based in Berlin. The photos in this book are from *Re:centering Periphery #2 – Moscow*, a documentary project by ogino:knauss consisting of Manuela Conti, Lorenzo Tripodi, Francesca Mizzoni, and Laura Colini www.oginoknauss.org/blog

NIKOLAOS PAPACHRISTODOU-LOU works as a consultant in the international development practice at ICF GHK in London. He has a background in economics and an MSc in Social Development from the Development Planning Unit (DPU) at University College London (UCL). Nikolaos' work focuses mainly on the integration of climate change adaptation into urban development policy and planning. The work addresses urbanization and urban social and economic development dynamics; climate change impacts, vulnerability and adaptation; and sustainable and climate-resilient urban development. Nikolaos has worked for clients including the World Bank, the Department for International Development (DfID), and local authorities. Recent projects have taken him to Brazil, Honduras, Nicaragua, Peru, Saint Lucia, Tanzania and Indonesia.

NICHOLAS A. PHELPS has a range of interests that cover economic and urban geography and planning internationally. His recent interests focus on the distinctive development of, politics in, and planning challenges facing, post-suburban communities internationally. He has long-standing interests in understanding the evolution of city-region economies. His recent work in the UK has focused on the politics and planning processes underlying the production of urban sprawl. Phelps' publications include *An Anatomy of Sprawl: Planning and Politics in Britain* (Routledge, 2012) and *International Perspectives on Suburbanization: a Post-suburban World?* (Palgrave-MacMillan, 2011), co-edited with Fulong Wu.

NATHAN SCHAFFER is a researcher, theorist, writer and artist. He is a recent graduate of the Masters in Environmental Studies (MES) program at York University, where his work centred on the political economy of urban space. For this, he conducted international research in Marseille, France, on their urban regeneration and development strategy *Euromediterranée* and its socio-political and economic symbiosis with the city's 2013 European Capital of Culture programme. As an artist and writer, Nathan has worked extensively in the advertising and creative sector, and continues to produce poetry and artwork exploring urban articulations of difference and symmetry.

SOPHIE SCHRAMM is an expert of urban sociotechnical infrastructure systems with a focus on the Global South. Her research concentrates on the interrelations between urban space and infrastructure systems, the dynamics and governance of urban and infrastructure development, as well as the role of planning under the condition of informality. In 2013 she finishes her dissertation thesis "City in flow – Hanoi's wastewater system in light of social and spatial transformations". Since April 2013, she works as a research associate at the chair for Spatial and Infrastructure Planning at the TU Darmstadt in the project "Translating urban infrastructure ideals and planning models: adaptation and creativity in water and sanitation systems in African cities", funded by the German Research Foundation (DFG).

ROB SHIELDS is H.M.Tory Chair and Professor as well as Director of the City Region Studies Centre at the University of Alberta. His work spans cultural theory, architecture and media studies to consider the relationships between social spaces and culture – processes of social spatialization, the governance of affect and outlook through planning and geographic spaces, and the development of cultural topologies that extend physical environments into meaningful milieux and cosmoses – *Ecologies of Affect*. This intellectual project is extended alongside colleagues, students and practitioners through the public research of University of Alberta City-Region Studies Centre. It is pursued through innovation with communities and professionals, in the creation of *Curb planning magazine*, books such as *Building Tomorrow, Places on the Margin, The Virtual* and the founding of *Space and Culture* an international peer-refereed journal.

FULONG WU is Bartlett Professor of Planning at the Bartlett School of Planning, University College London. His research interests include spatial structure, housing and land development, China's urbanism and urban development, urban and regional governance, urban poverty, and social spatial differentiation. He has an extensive record of publications including being co-editor (with Laurence Ma) of *Restructuring the Chinese City* (Routledge, 2005), editor of *Globalization and the Chinese City* (Routledge, 2006), editor of *China's Emerging Cities: The Making of New Urbanism* (Routledge, 2007), and co-author (with Jiang Xu and Anthony Gar-On Yeh) of *Urban Development in Post-Reform China: State, Market, and Space* (Routledge, 2007), co-author (with Chris Webster, Shenjing He, and Yuting Liu) of *Urban Poverty in China* (Edward Elgar, 2010), co-editor (with Chris Webster) of *Marginalization in Urban China* (Palgrave Macmillan, 2010), and co-editor (with Nick Phelps) of *Comparative Suburbanism* (Palgrave Macmillan, 2010), and recently co-editor (with Fangzhu Zhang, Chris Webster, Routledge, 2013) of *Rural Migrants in Urban China*.

Teaching at York University, **DOUGLAS YOUNG**'s interest is in undertaking critical urban research. His goal is to interpret empirical phenomena in ways that challenge mainstream concepts and analyses. Underlying this approach is a belief that a progressive urban future is possible. Currently, Young's research is in two broad areas: The first is processes of decline and renewal in post-war suburban districts. He is exploring the discursive, material and policy dimensions of those processes as well as the intersecting roles of state, market and civil society actors. This research is being undertaken in Toronto and Leipzig. The second area of research is a consideration of how we live in the 21st century with the legacies of 20th century urbanisms, more specifically socialist and modernist urbanisms. This research is a comparative study of iconic spaces in Hanoi, Berlin and Stockholm and is funded by a SSHRC Standard Research Grant.

© 2013 by jovis Verlag GmbH
Texts by kind permission of the authors.
Pictures by kind permission of the photographers/
holders of the picture rights.

Cover design: Susanne Rösler, Berlin; photographs by
ogino:knauss, Roger Keil and Shubhra Gururani

Design and setting: Susanne Rösler, Berlin
Lithography: Bild1Druck, Berlin
Printing and binding: GRASPO CZ, a.s., Zlín

Bibliographic information published by the
Deutsche Nationalbibliothek
The Deutsche Nationalbibliothek lists this publication in
the Deutsche Nationalbibliografie; detailed bibliographic
data are available on the Internet at
http://dnb.d-nb.de

jovis Verlag GmbH
Kurfürstenstrasse 15/16
10785 Berlin

www.jovis.de

ISBN 978-3-86859-231-3